INTERNATIONAL FOOTBALL BOOK
No. 15

The Spirit of Liverpool '73 – it's two on one, but when that one is Liverpool's John Toshack (right) it means he gets that inch or two higher, and carves out a goal chance against West Ham.

INTERNATIONAL FOOTBALL BOOK

No. 15

Edited by Stratton Smith

Contributing Editors

ERIC BATTY

PETER JONES

with contributions by

FRANZ BECKENBAUER   SIR MATT BUSBY   JOHAN CRUYFF

GUNTER NETZER   CHARLIE GEORGE

PETER LORIMER   PETER OSGOOD   ALFREDO DI STEFANO

STEVE PERRYMAN   MARTIN BUCHAN

MIKE SUMMERBEE   MALCOLM MACDONALD   BRYAN 'POP' ROBSON

HELMUT SCHOEN   MANUEL VELAZQUEZ

KAROL DOBIAS   ED STEWART   JAIME GRACA

KARL-HEINZ HEIMANN   GEOFFREY GREEN

FRANCOIS THEBAUD   BRIAN GLANVILLE   ANTAL DUNAI

GORDON JEFFERY

SOUVENIR PRESS LTD   ·   LONDON

First published 1973 by Souvenir Press Ltd., 95 Mortimer Street,
London WIN 8HP, and simultaneously in Canada by J. M.
Dent & Son (Canada) Ltd., Ontario, Canada.

ISBN 0 285 62100 9

Filmset by Keyspools Ltd., Golborne, Lancs.
Printed in Great Britain by
C. Tinling & Co. Ltd., Prescot and London.

CONTENTS

5

CONTENTS

LIST OF ILLUSTRATIONS

Three of the men (top, right) who have helped create the new West Germany skip through a training routine; (left to right) Uli Hoeness, Paul Breitner, and Gunter Netzer. (Below) An important fourth man – manager Helmut Schoen.

MEN, NOT STYLE, CREATE

'NEW' WEST GERMANY

BY HELMUT SCHOEN
West Germany's National
team Manager

ONE of the most difficult tasks I have faced to date with the German national team was our European Championship quarter-final match against England at Wembley. There were however favourable indications for us in that in England I knew we were expected to play defensively. Luckily, we had the kind of players available who can take advantage of such a situation and therefore we approached the game with confidence.

Playing away from home, the visitors are usually expected to be more defensive and though it is not always true – it differs according to the individual circumstances of each game – it is therefore sometimes easier to win away than it is at home. This is because when playing at home our opponents, being the visitors, play with a more defensive attitude and this makes goalscoring more difficult.

Before the first of the two games against England we planned to take control of midfield. We had nothing to lose in any case by attempting to control the game. Rather than give England the initiative by falling back in strength on our goal we decided to try and gain control of the game in the centre of the pitch. *This is the key to top-class football today; giving the impression that football is less defensive, though this is often only an illusion.*

We planned to take the initiative at Wembley right from the start. Thanks to the wonderful morale of our players, and their skills, we were successful. It would however be misleading to suggest that we knew we could beat England at Wembley, though we set out to try.

In my opinion, it is still one of the most formidable tasks for any national team to win at Wembley. It will continue to be so for the foreseeable future. Any team that beats England at Wembley has reason to be well satisfied with their performance and I was very proud of my players when we achieved it.

This Wembley victory and our final elimination of England went some way to redressing our great disappointment when we were beaten there in the Final of the 1966 World Cup. On that occasion the turning point came when Hurst scored a highly speculative goal for England, hitting the ball against our crossbar. I don't want to open old wounds or start again the old arguments, but I must

say I would never have given a goal in such circumstances. But at the time, my players and I accepted the referee's decision as we must always do.

Our present team is a very fine one, but it does not differ in style from the traditional German game as much as some people seem to think it does. We had a very good team in the 1966 World Cup and it was even stronger in the 1970 competition. Since then, several key players have been replaced. I refer in particular to Willi Schulz and Uwe Seeler, who have retired from international football, and Wolfgang Overath.

Overath was injured rather badly after the World Cup in Mexico, where he helped us into third place. Following an operation, he is getting back to his best form and he remains a member of the national team squad even though he missed the big successes of 1972 in the European Championship.

The team that won that Trophy, beating Belgium and the Soviet Union in the final stages, evolved first from the basis of the excellent team we had in Mexico plus Gunter Netzer and several other new young players. Netzer had been a member of the squad before the last World Cup but sustained a very curious injury. It was not serious, a strain in his thigh, but it took more than three months to heal and so I nominated Helmut Haller to replace him in the team.

For the European Championship, with Haller and Karl-Heinz Schnellinger playing in Italy, Overath and Berti Vogts among others unavailable through injury, we had to find several new players. Naturally the first place I looked was to our two leading clubs FC Bayern Munchen and Borussia Moenchengladbach. Fortunately, the players we needed were readily available within these two teams and so the side that won at Wembley and

A helpful hint for the West German goalkeepers (not the strongest men in the squad!), Volkmar Gross and Sepp Maier, from manager Schoen.

finally won the European Championship just fell into place.

Since playing in Mexico, we have maintained our own German style of play, but I think improved it, too. Today, our team is more homogeneous – more of a complete team rather than individuals – but still essentially German in style, and with all the qualities of dedication, determination, discipline, and sportsmanship which we have always insisted upon.

In Germany, there is a very good set-up between myself as the national coach and the club coaches of the teams in the *Bundesliga*. We meet regularly and discuss the problems concerning technique, tactics, and organisation that affect us all. We have a very friendly understanding of each others' problems and duties. I would like to have all the players in the national squad for training together more often. As much is done as we can within the limitations imposed by the needs of the clubs, whose fixture lists are now more crowded than ever before.

The day at Wembley when England learned all about West Germany, and particularly about Gunter Netzer (top), sharing a joke with manager Schoen. (Below) Agony for Gordon Banks as he is beaten by Netzer's penalty. (Facing page) Gerd Muller dances back to help out German defender Paul Breitner, being pressed by Francis Lee and Colin Bell.

Our major task now is to prepare for the 1974 World Cup, in which we will be the host country. I am sure it will be a great success and I very much hope that we can win the Trophy. It is very important for a variety of reasons to play a World Cup at home. I would say that it was probably the decisive factor when England won the World Cup in 1966, and I certainly hope that we can do it next year.

We have had a very good team for some years. Remember we reached the Final in 1966 and earned third place in 1970 and our team is I think a better balanced side now. Therefore it is reasonable to hope that unless we are handicapped by serious injury to key players we have every chance of success.

Between now and the first ball being kicked in 1974, however, a great deal can change. Among the 16 Finalists there will be a number of good teams and it would be a grave mistake to be complacent. I am sure that several of the Finalists will have a good chance of winning the World Cup, though as I look at the situation now we do not even know who the other 14 teams will be.

At the moment only Brazil (as holders) and ourselves are sure to take part, and we must wait and see who qualifies. One thing is for sure. There will be one or two teams that will surprise everyone with the quality of their football. Every World Cup staged so far has produced surprise teams, and I feel sure that 1974 will be no exception.

'We haven't Brazilians' high gifts'

BY FRANZ BECKENBAUER
captain of West Germany
and F.C. Bayern Munich

A BLEND OF WHAT'S BEST IN EUROPEAN FOOTBALL

IN my time with Bayern we've had four different trainers (or managers, as they may be known in some other countries) and they've all had one thing in common. They have all encouraged ball players, or what I would call *playing* players, which has been fortunate for me. I'm not the kind that enjoys tearing about in training, sprinting, gymnastics, and the like. I prefer to play with the ball, stroking it about and caressing it. The ball and I are very good friends, and I'd like to keep it that way.

Although the emphasis in German football is now on skill, we are by no means Brazilians and don't pretend to be. They are altogether much more gifted in terms of technique – but we are, I think, a blend of what is best in European football. I enjoy playing and I'm sure I speak for all my colleagues both in my Club and the national team when I say

we get a great deal of satisfaction from presenting what we feel is something like top-class football.

The game has changed a lot in my time, of course. I began as a centre-forward and later I played wing-half in the old 'WM' system. There was no *libero* or *ausputzer*, as we call the free-back in Germany. Only a stopper centre-half. It was the Bayern boss Zlatko 'Tschik' Cajkowski who converted me, moving me to play the stopper game one day when our centre-half got injured.

I enjoyed it right away and I believe I can contribute more to the game, playing at the back of the defence. From there you can see the whole field better than anyone else (except the goalkeeper). With the freedom to come forward any time you choose you can be the master of the match, controlling everything. Certainly I wouldn't want to play

FOOTBALL SWORD
OF HONOUR 1973

FRANZ BECKENBAUER

*'For distinguished service to
British and international football*

anywhere else now.

The way I now play I am the last man in the defence but also the first man in attack. Playing at the back gives me all the opportunities I need to use my skill and I'm sure I couldn't play better in any other position. It has been said that the English should copy we Germans now, but in my opinion, no team should copy another. Everyone would be best advised to develop their own game, their own style of play. Having said that, I do think the English generally should improve their skills and become a bit more technical in their approach. Strength and speed, which the English have always had, are no longer enough today.

England, of course, have a lot of good players. I'm sure they can do better than they did against us at Wembley and in Berlin, when we last met. English players have wonderful physical condition and we Germans still have the greatest respect for them. With all the good players available England could certainly be a strong candidate for the World Cup next year, if the emphasis is placed on skill rather than strength.

I am often asked what I think of my club-mate, Gerdi Muller. My immediate reactions are two. First, I think his goalscoring figures speak for themselves. Secondly, I'm very glad he plays with me and not against me. Muller's biggest assets are his tenacity and quick reactions. He doesn't score goals from 25 or 30 yards as Uwe Seeler did, but inside the penalty area he is deadly. Some of Muller's goals are quite fantastic. I've seen him score even when surrounded by three or four defenders simply because his reflexes and reactions are so quick. He just leaves everyone flat-footed.

FOOTBALL SWORD OF HONOUR 1973

Muller got one of the goals in the most exciting match I've ever played in; that day in Leon when we beat England 3–2 after extra time, during the 1970 World Cup in Mexico. When we were losing 0–2 we all thought our chance had gone. I think perhaps England made a mistake when they took off Bobby Charlton. First Seeler and then Muller got the vital goals and we were back in the game.

That was a wonderful feeling, to win that day; but just a few days later I was made to realise just how the English players felt when we in turn lost to Italy in the semi-finals. Within three days I experienced the joys of winning a big match which I thought was lost, and then being beaten in a game I though we had won.

Certainly, it was an exciting game – but it was a terrible disappointment to lose 4–3 to Italy after extra time. To get so close to the Final, and then lose after being in front was the biggest disappointment I've ever known in football.

Next year we have a great chance of winning the World Cup. Playing in your own country is a tremendous advantage and this is my greatest ambition left in football – to be a member of the German team in 1974, and help to win the Trophy.

BECKENBAUER : 'SUPREME HALLMARK OF GREATNESS'

WHEN Franz Beckenbauer first figured prominently on the world stage it was as an orthodox wing-half during the 1966 World Cup. English critics were enthusiastic about his creative skills but dubious about his defensive qualities, not knowing at the time that he was already permanently installed as his Club's stopper.

Certainly it seemed that he was too good a player to be wasted as a stopper centre-half and, indeed, he was never entirely limited to that role. Nothing about his play for Bayern Munchen at that time indicated that he would play a leading part in revolutionising the role of the super-defensive player . . . the Italian *libero*.

Beckenbauer's contribution to the evolving West German game has been enormous and his sorties upfield have led to a new concept in defensive play. From his position behind the defence he comes forward, with and without the ball, to have a really decisive influence on the play in midfield and

BY ERIC BATTY

attack. Even, at times, going right forward to score goals himself.

His new role is perhaps best described as the old attacking centre-half of pre-'WM' days when the old number five was the key man in attack. The last of the old-style attacking centre-halves was Ernst Ocwirk of Austria, who starred in the 1954 World Cup and was nicknamed 'Clockwork', because he made the Austrians tick.

Beckenbauer now assumes a similar role for Bayern Munchen and West Germany and brings to the most destructive of all positions a class and flair possessed by few top international forwards. At a stroke he has out-dated the term *libero*, or *ausputzer* as the free-back is known in Germany, and created a new role that has thus far defied description. An attacking *libero* is a clear contradiction

'Beckenbauer recalls the . . . legend of Fritz Walter, captain of the 1954 World Cup-winning team'; Walter in action (left) in that Final against Hungary's centre-half Gyula Lorant. (Right) Sepp Maier – though often criticised – shows he can't be faulted for courage at least; he beats off challenges from England's Colin Bell and Martin Peters.

in terms, though that is precisely the way Beckenbauer plays, covering in defence when needed, but always eager to move forward at every opportunity.

Willingness to go forward would be welcome enough in these days of defence-orientated tactics but Beckenbauer's skill and intelligence is such that his influence permeates through the entire team and when he has an off-day the effect is felt everywhere.

Unruffled calm and superb skills are the hallmarks of Beckenbauer's game. His intelligent positioning and anticipation enable him to provide cover in defence, winning the ball usually with interception rather than tackling, and once in possession his distribution is near perfection. Although only moderate in the air and with a definite preference for doing everything with his right foot, he plays with the inside and outside of his one 'stick' like a master craftsman.

If opponents attempt to get up tight and dispossess him, he sends them the wrong way with a

feint; if they stand off he purveys superbly-laid passes and flights them in such a way that they 'swing' in the air, curling away from the opponent and turning back to drop precisely at the feet of a colleague. Even to get up close within a yard or two is no answer, for Beckenbauer also has that much admired weapon – the chip – and even with a dead ball he can lift the ball high over an opponent's head and drop it down almost immediately.

Such skills as he displays are confined to legitimate World-class stars and his performances throughout the past two years have been such that managers all over the world are now thinking in terms of putting their most skilful and intelligent player, once the midfield general, back behind the defenders *à la Beckenbauer*. There can be no higher praise than that – to have the entire world copying you.

In his sorties upfield Beckenbauer recalls the craftsmen of old, the Mannions, Carters and, in Germany, the legend of Fritz Walter, captain of the 1954 World Cup-winning team. Moving forward he ghosts past opponents; side-stepping, shuffling, giving off a pass here, taking the ball back there, the confident, competent, commander of all he surveys.

Capable of creating havoc in midfield, Beckenbauer also possesses the supreme hallmark of greatness, the ability to lay the perfect through pass that sets a colleague clear for a direct run to goal, unopposed. Inch-perfect passes, allied to supreme timing, and the gift of disguising his intentions until the penetrating ball has been despatched.

Even a Soccer giant is just 'one of the team' in his family's own backyard – Franz Beckenbauer relaxes (left) with wife Brigitte and sons (by descending size and age!) Michael, Thomas, and baby Stefan. (Top right) Franz Beckenbauer . . . 'executioner par excellence' . . . beats England's Bobby Moore and Roy McFarland in Berlin.

But Beckenbauer's achievements are not limited to creation. He is also an executioner *par excellence*, scorer of many fine and vital goals. None was more important perhaps than his superb matchwinner against England during the 1970 World Cup in Mexico when, with the score at 2–2 in extra time, Beckenbauer dribbled past three defenders like a downhill skier on the slalom and scored the winning goal with a superbly-placed right-foot cross shot.

A world-class star at 20, Beckenbauer is now, at 27, within striking distance of Uwe Seeler's all-time record number of 72 international appearances for West Germany. Only serious injury can prevent him from joining the elite band who have represented their country more than 100 times. But whatever the future holds for him, Beckenbauer will be best remembered as the player who brought class and skill to the most destructive role that modern Soccer has seen – the Italian style *libero*.

THE most exhilarating and satisfying experience I have known so far in football was helping my country win the European Championship in 1972 but the Final, exciting though it was, takes second place in my memory to our wonderful win over England at Wembley. That of course was at the quarter-final stage and was perhaps the most critical of all games for us; even more important than the Final itself, in some ways.

I like English football. There are a lot of fantastic players in England, though not many of them play for the national team. Some of the best are Irish, like Georgie Best; but I've always admired Bobby Charlton, and I liked Martin Chivers when I first saw him. Of course, it's another kind of game, with more fighting, but I like it just the same.

Somehow, I feel sure that England could do better in the big international competitions; but I don't see enough of English football to be able to explain what is wrong. All I can say is that they ought to be more successful, on the evidence of what I have seen.

Maybe something has to be changed in the English way of thinking about the game. Personally, I like the technical players rather than the fighters – players with really outstanding skill. Maybe the

++

'draft new men

now . . . or miss

out at Munich'

++

FIND THE WINGERS, AND ENGLAND WILL BE GREAT

English people as a whole like more some kind of 'fighting football', I don't know; but I feel sure they would do better if they gave the *technicals* a real opportunity to show what they can do.

Above all, I feel sure the English national team must make one change. They should have at least one winger in their team always, and preferably two. Then I think England would once more be a real power. This doesn't mean that I think England's days of glory are over. They will still be a

ence. Even the younger players have the experience of being successful in big competitions and that of course breeds confidence and the determination to be successful again. These are vital ingredients in any team that aims for the biggest prize in world football.

Of course our team was very strong in Mexico, too, though I personally didn't play in the 1970 World Cup. I had played for the national team in the important period before Mexico but as every-

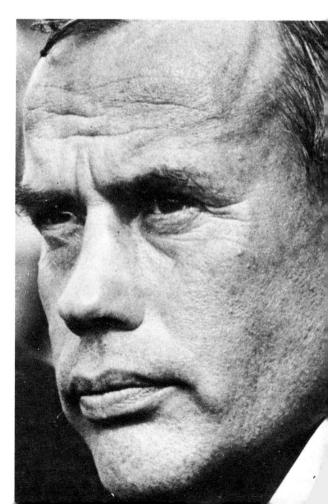

BY GUNTER NETZER
Borussia Moenchengladbach
and West Germany
---

very difficult side to beat in the next World Cup, even if they don't change. But being difficult to beat does not make winners. That is quite different.

The England team we played at Wembley and beat 3–1 was basically the same side that played in the World Cup in Mexico and so far there is no indication that new players are being drafted into the side. This, I believe, will be of critical importance in the next World Cup. There are still too many old players in the England team and if they remain in the team they could be too old in 1974.

We are more fortunate in this respect in West Germany, for though we have a very good team now, and have already been successful, the present team's average age will still be only 29 when the next World Cup comes around. That I think is about the right balance between youth and experi-

Hennes Weisweiler, manager-coach of the tremendous Borussia Moenchengladbach Club . . . 'Being with him for nearly ten years has been of great importance to me and my game' says Netzer.

one must know, I had a misunderstanding with our manager Mr. Helmut Schoen some months before. Though that had been settled amicably three months before the World Cup, I was rather badly injured. I had a strange muscular injury to my left thigh that gave me trouble for more than three months and was very slow to heal.

So I couldn't play in the critical period before Mexico and lost the chance to appear there. This is why our successes at Wembley and in the final stages of the Championship in Belgium were doubly pleasing for me.

I'm sure we have an excellent chance of success next·year when the World Cup is played in Germany, but strange things happen. The home team usually does well because of all the natural advantages, and of course we have a good team, too. We

I have a very busy life with many interests outside the game. I own a restaurant, a discotheque, and have an insurance agency and a public relations firm. Football remains my great interest and takes most of my time. The game comes first with me. All the time.

I haven't travelled enough to be as well informed about the game in other countries as I would like. Of course it is impossible when you have to train almost every day and play in League matches every week. But I think the game elsewhere has much in common with our game in Germany.

(Top) George Best, also 'Highest bracket' . . . but on extended (!) holiday just now, seen here with ex-Bunny Linda Joinett in Palm Springs, California. (Below) The one and only Edson Arantes do Nascimento – 'Pele' – a player whose career survived extraordinary pressures and closes with dignity and honour.

should do well – I'm sure we can – but there will be strong opposition and one never knows.

England will be strong, for sure – maybe if they change a few things they could be very strong indeed. I think Italy, too, could be very useful and a big threat to us. They also have some very fine players and I would put their inside-forward Gianni Rivera in the highest bracket, along with our Franz Beckenbauer, Pele, and Best.

The South Americans have a lot of good players, particularly the Brazilians, but I don't feel any of the South American teams will be a big threat next year. They can all play very good football, and they do . . . in South America. But they don't seem to be very good travellers. I may be wrong, but in my opinion Brazil are not half as good in Europe as they are in South America. They just don't seem able to compete successfully against European teams in European conditions. In short – they cannot play European football.

Giovanni Rivera (top left) of AC Milan and Italy . . . 'I put him in the highest bracket' says Netzer. (Below) Colin Bell of England skirmishes with the 'German Peril' – Netzer, on ground, and Beckenbauer.

Bad moment for Switzerland 'keeper Mario Prosperi – Gunter Netzer strides in to score in West German's 5–1 win (above). (Right) Bad moment for Ipswich centre-half Hunter, beaten in this challenge from former Manchester United star George Best.

I've played all my life in Moenchengladbach. I was playing here as a boy for 1st FC Moenchengladbach – an amateur of course – when Kurt Langner invited me to join Borussia. I have never regretted moving and owe the club and my coach, Mr. Hennes Weisweiler, a very great deal. Mr. Weisweiler is, I am sure, one of the best football brains in the game and being with him for nearly ten years now has been of great importance to me and my game.

I don't really like the fighters in football, though we have them here, too. Every time I put my boots on to play I know before the game that I am going to be knocked down many times. I get kicks and fouls but what can I do? It's part of the game and you just have to accept it. All I can do is make up my mind to play my game as well as I can. There is a referee to decide what is fair and what is not fair, and I can only hope that he decides right.

By ALFREDO DI STEFANO
former Real Madrid star, now manager of Valencia C.F.

MANY people have been misled into believing that sides like Ajax and the West German national team are playing more attacking football than has been the case for some years. I will not argue that they are not playing a more attractive style of play – more interesting to watch – but in my opinion they are just as defensive-minded.

The difference is that they defend in a different way, using their skill to keep the ball so that the other team cannot attack. The game generally has

'They're just
as defensive'

The familiar, stocky figure of Alfred Di Stefano, now a manager, but still training. (Right) Di Stefano relaxes in Valencia . . . 'even grandmothers now know something about the game'.

DON'T LET GERMANY AND AJAX FOOL YOU

become more defence-minded to provide more security for the players and coaches, bringing continuity and success.

I am sure there is more interest in the game today than ever before – even grandmothers now know something about the game. Every man under the age of 90 has at least some interest in the game and the majority go to watch live football at least a few times in their lives.

Football has become a part of modern living and if attendances are lower now in some countries then I am sure this is due to the influence of televised football. Their team's game being shown on TV will not deter the passionate fans from going to see the game; but it will, perhaps, persuade some people to stay at home and watch in the comfort of their home who might otherwise have gone to the ground.

Make no mistakes about Ajax and West Germany. They have fewer goals scored against them than the majority of teams in Spain or South America. The difference is that they have exceptionally highly-

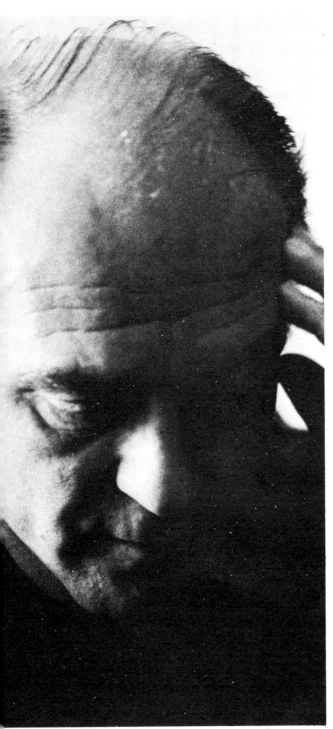

skilled players who are equally good whether defending or attacking. Their players also have good physical qualities, morale, and the mental approach that is required for winning competitive football today.

I have heard it suggested that Argentinian teams are dirty, but this was not my feeling when I worked there as manager of Boca Juniors. Football is not played at top level by a bunch of charity-minded nuns, but the Argentinians are no more dirty or less sporting than anyone else. This opinion will probably clash with that of many English fans who have seen Estudiantes and the Racing Club play in Britain in World Club Championship games. But these matches create exceptional circumstances and they should not be taken as the general guide.

In any case, there are two sides to every coin and if English players or fans think that the Argentinians are dirty players I can assure you that the Argentinians feel exactly the same. That is to say, everyone in Buenos Aires is firmly convinced that the dirtiest players they ever saw came from England! At the same time, the Argentines still have a very great respect for English football.

Believe me, I saw many fine players two years ago when I was manager of Boca Juniors. Good players spring up like mushrooms in the Argentine and some of them are extraordinary. But there is a problem with so many good players – it destroys continuity.

What happens is that a new young player suddenly springs up and attracts attention. The fans are always looking for new idols – but there is an economic factor which causes problems for the clubs. Once the new star is established he naturally wants to be paid more. But the clubs are in financial difficulties and the majority would like to transfer their stars.

This is simply explained. The star gets very well paid but because there are many good young players he is easily replaced. So the club is financially better off if they can transfer the star, receiving a transfer fee, and use another player who gets a smaller salary. This destroys continuity, which is very important from the manager's point of view.

There is nothing better than an established side of good players that stay together as a unit for a few years, but the economics of the game make this a really difficult problem for the majority of clubs in the Argentine.

I was lucky enough in my playing career to have played alongside many good players, some of them exceptional. I would specially mention Gento, Rial, Puskas, Marsal, Del Sol, and Kopa. They were all good players, each with his own characteristics, his own special qualities. That makes comparison and rating them '1-2-3', etc., very difficult if not impossible.

The best forward line I ever saw was not Real Madrid's but that of the Argentine club River Plate during the 1940's. That attack was phenomenal: Munoz, Moreno, Pedernera, Lahuna, Loustau . . . the fans and newspapers referred to River at that time as the 'goalscoring-machine'.

I have no regrets about my own playing career. Each era has its own specialities, its own peculiarities. But the game goes up and down in public esteem. Everyone has his prime, his best period, and in a sport where youth is the key factor you have to be fatalistic.

If intelligence and skills were the only important elements in a game like football it would change the game completely. The key factors in Soccer are speed and strength and that means: Youth. I look back to my youth with pleasure and satisfaction. It is enough for me that I have been a footballer.

Now that I am a manager, I appreciate the game even more than I did when I was playing. They are truly wonderful, these many new facets. Being a manager or coach is a challenge and full of surprises. You never know what tomorrow can bring; emotion, happiness, disappointment. But I am happy to still be in the game, content to accept whatever tomorrow brings.

I really am convinced it is still possible, in what is basically a tough business, to play entertaining football and still be successful in terms of results.

The key of course is good training and good players, with each individual being a high-class player familiar with his tasks and duties yet able to play a part in a team game with his colleagues. It is easier to play in some ways today because the athletic preparation is better, for example. So too are the medical facilities for the treatment of injuries, and so on.

Manager Di Stefano relaxes with his wife and three children in their Valencia home.

THREE TOP INTERNATIONAL CRITICS LOOK
AT THE WORLD CUP—AND ARE UNANIMOUS,

IT'S GERMANY !

1. GEOFFREY GREEN

THE TIMES, LONDON

SPORTING journalists everywhere live on a trampoline of nails. We bounce from one mistaken view to the next and end up punctured as a sieve. Finally, none of our opinions hold water.

It's all good for the soul no doubt and as the song writer says: 'There's no need for turning back, all roads lead to where we stand, and we must walk them all, no matter what we may have planned.'

We've all had our small successes from time to time, but in a curious way they are more embarassing and certainly shorter lived than any gross ill-judgement. Few people, for instance, let me forget that I forecast Italy as the World Champions of 1966. They were immediately eliminated by little North Korea, the 'diddy-men' of the Competition.

Last season I gave Newcastle United to win the F.A. Cup. What happens? They were knocked out by Hereford United, rank outsiders, and at that time not even members of the Football League. Recently nine people out of ten forecast Joe Frazier to retain his crown as heavyweight boxing Champion of the world. Almost inevitably, he hit the canvas six times inside the opening two rounds to be knocked out by a young tornado named George Foreman.

So it is on these terms of loser take all (on the chin)

that I predict West Germany to win in Munich 1974 and become Football Champions of the world for the second time in precisely twenty years.

Not that this is an original opinion. Almost certainly they will start as favourites with everything in their favour. The challenge is to find someone to beat them and with nearly 18 months still to go the problem is as complicated as a nest of Chinese boxes.

First, I shall exclude the South Americans–vaunted Brazil, the holders, Champions three times since the war and Finalists on four occasions since 1950. Certainly their fantasy and poetic feel for the game remains in men like Tostaõ, Paulo Cesar, Rivelino, Jairzinho and others. But with the retirement of Pelé–'O Rei', the king–I suspect something will have departed from their emotional soul.

The Brazilians still pick footballers off trees like beautiful, ripe apples. Yet this time, I think, European functionalism will be the master and this goes for other challengers from the New World like Uruguay, Argentine, and Peru, one of the exciting new forces to emerge in Mexico three years ago.

No, it is the Old World that should have the last word on this occasion and here I would welcome the emergence of either The Netherlands, Belgium, or Yugoslavia to supplement the traditional spirit of England and the Latin flair of Italy.

England's World Cup hopes stagger from a Welsh upper-cut at Wembley: Wales held England to a 1–1 draw and left Sir Alf Ramsey's men under pressure to win both their remaining qualifying matches against Poland to be certain of a place in the Finals. (Top) Welsh 'keeper Gary Sprake's

only defeat – a 25-yard 'scorcher' from Leeds' team-mate Norman Hunter. (Below) England striker Rodney Marsh floored by Wales' John Roberts but (inset) Marsh is on his feet again to celebrate Hunter's equaliser.

The Dutch, in particular, have at last found themselves through the successes of Ajax and Feyenoord in the European Cup over the past three years. They have many finely toned and skilled players like Cruyff, Van Hanegem, Neeskens, Krol, Suurbier, and Keizer to call upon and now that they have found a new appetite for the fame and financial rewards that go with the 'big time' they could mount a threat.

The same could go for Belgium with men like Van Himst, Van Moer, Devrindt, and Semmeling in their ranks. And remember they knocked Italy out of the European Nations Championship last season.

All these are in the race. But it is West Germany who should reach the winning post first. The ball is in their court. Their home terrain; overwhelming support on the terraces; abounding nationalism; and, above all, their all-round cohesion as a side of true class.

Already reigning Champions of Europe, their biggest danger will be to hold their form and avoid staleness. Excused–as hosts–the burden of having to qualify from a dog-fight, they have meanwhile set themselves, with typical Germanic thoroughness, a tough programme of preparation.

As a build-up to the final stages Helmut Schöen, their manager, planned 19 internationals over the final 18 months (one of these, last November, saw Switzerland swamped 5–1, with four goals claimed by Gerd Müller, the executioner). In this list are included matches with Brazil and Argentine and when these are done we should know how well the Germans are flexing their muscles. But, to say it again, their big problem is to retain their resilience.

I think they will do it. Six of their current side belong to Bayern Munich and that offers teamwork and vital understanding as an invaluable foundation. Beyond that in players like the elegant Beckenbauer, Netzer, Breitner, Hoeness, Wimmer, and Müller they possess a stable of classic proportions.

The side that beats them will have fully earned the World Cup of 1974. But I remember Italy 1966 and Newcastle United 1972 . . .

WHO will win the next World Cup? If I knew that – if I was able to forecast with absolute certainty the results of single games, even in the French League, I would not be a journalist but a millionaire. But football isn't like that, it has too much in common with life itself and defies any mathematical certainties. And in the World Cup there are many games, not just the Final.

However, if **WEST GERMANY** look to be the obvious favourite, I would like to make one thing clear: That my one hope is that the most attacking team will be crowned World Champions in Munich.

No matter how you look at it the Germans stand out one year before the final stages. They have the best players, the best technique, the best team; and every indication is that they will repeat their triumph of 1954 at the Wankdorf Stadium in Berne.

marked by their feeble performances in the Mini-Cup they staged the same year; and the ground advantage which accrues to Helmut Schoen's team in the next World Cup; all give the same indication.

Ground advantage and an outstanding team are not always decisive factors, however. To put these factors in doubt it is only necessary to recall the 1950 series when Brazil staged the tournament and after some brilliant attacking football reached the Final. There, at their own Maracaña Stadium in Rio de Janeiro, with 200,000 of their supporters looking on, Brazil went down 2–1 to Uruguay. Ground advantage is not necessarily decisive.

BRAZIL, of course, should never be under-estimated. They will be touring Europe in 1973 and we shall be able to judge their chances better after

2. FRANCOIS THEBAUD

MIROIR DU FOOTBALL, PARIS

But in football nothing is certain, and this is particularly true in the World Cup. The Germans themselves underlined this when they beat the Hungarian *Wunderteam*, the hottest favourites of all time, in the 1954 Final. Moreover, in the pre-liminary-round matches of that same Competition in 1954, Hungary beat West Germany by eight goals to three – but less than three weeks later they went down 2–3 to the Germans in the Final.

A year before the kick-off everything points to the Germans. Their brilliant success in the European *Coupe des Nations* in 1972; the regression of Brazil;

Francois Thebaud.

their games over here. But if we take as a guide the number of goals scored in the 1972 Brazilian Championship, won by Palmeiras of Saõ Paulo, it is clear that even in Brazil the tendency towards defensive play has been accentuated.

It remains to be seen if, during the qualifying

'IF YOU LOVE FOOTBALL, IT HAS TO BE WEST GERMANY'

Gary Sprake, a Welsh hero at Wembley, saves from Eng-land's Martin Chivers (right), with centre-half Mike England in close support.

rounds, another challenger can be developed in Europe. With more than a year to work in and make changes it is possible that one of several European teams could improve to challenge Germany and Brazil as favourites.

This kind of revelation is, however, highly improbable in the context of modern football. The game everywhere is characterised by negative tactics – the 'counter-attack' system based on a reinforced defence *(beton a l'Italienne)* . . . or the overpopulated midfield system adopted by **ENGLAND** and Brazil. Both systems work to prevent what the game needs – the development of outstanding individual players.

The German team today is actually the most attacking team in the world because Beckenbauer is not a true free-back. He plays under false colours and actually reinforces an already very good midfield pair in Netzer and Wimmer. But even the weight of Beckenbauer, Netzer, and Wimmer would not be enough if Schoen imitates Sir Alf Ramsey and deprives his team of the presence of real wingers. The Germans' real strength lies in their wingers, Heynckes and Kremers, who attack on both flanks like tidal waves.

Brazil, on the other hand, have only one winger, Jairzinho, and today they play the counter-attacking game as have England since 1966. It is wingers

(Left) Josef 'Jupp' Heynckes of Borussia Moenchengladbach . . . 'The Germans' real strength lies in their wingers'; (top) Jairzinho of Brazil in action against Uruguay . . . 'Brazil's only winger'.

that play the decisive role in football today.

If none of the established football countries decides to abandon the current defence-orientated tactics then it is to be hoped for all those that love real football – inconceivable without creative ability in attack – that the Germans win the World Cup. This assumes that the Germans will not abandon one of their wingers, and retain within their team the characteristics they showed in 1972.

This would truly be a victory for attacking football – and good for the game as a whole – for the Germans are an attacking team at present. It may not seem so with a *libero* behind the defence, but their tactical organisation is ambiguous. There is all the difference in the world between an Italian-style *libero* and the way that Franz Beckenbauer plays.

Still, I hope others will follow the Germans' lead. With a year to go anything is possible. If it is true that football has developed, it is also still developing, and its evolution depends on factors outside the game. Much depends on the attitude of society as a whole. If the fans stay away from matches in England or **ITALY** then the clubs will be forced to play more attacking football and so would their respective national teams.

It looks like West Germany, but in an unstable world it would be presumptuous to suppose that even the unlikely is impossible in this modern world. I still hope for a general return to attacking football in 1974.

3. KARL-HEINZ HEIMANN

DER KICKER, MUNICH

A S a German, writing about the next World Cup it should be very easy for me. For more than a year most of the world and all of Europe has been saying that **WEST GERMANY** will win the 1974 World Cup. That, at least, is the assessment of the best-known and most-respected football experts. This being so, why shouldn't I, as a German, simply echo the others?

Erwin Kremers, outside-left of Schalke '04 and West Germany . . . 'Heynckes and Kremers attack on both flanks like tidal waves'.

If the World Cup had been played last autumn I would have had no hesitation in betting on Germany. The Brazilians would still have been imponderables, an unknown quantity capable of pulling off a surprise; but it would have been Germany all the way. No doubt.

But my experience of following football has made me cautious. Changes can take place almost overnight. Within a very short space of time anything can happen, and I am keeping a watchful eye on **BRAZIL**, particularly, after their showing in the Mini-Cup last summer. It's difficult for us old hands to imagine Brazil playing without Pelé. We shall just have to wait and see.

There is no doubt the German national team must be reckoned one of the favourites. Its style of play is refreshing, the teamwork completely harmonious; and the individual standard in terms of technique and tactics is manifold. No doubt they may stand up against the best in the world. But I use the word 'may' advisedly, because in football, as I have already indicated, nothing is guaranteed. Nothing can be taken for granted.

The absolute quality of the German team I take for granted. That is an established fact, because every player has such a high level of technical and sporting intelligence and skill. They are interchangeable and able to vary their game and tactics to suit the circumstances; if necessary, to switch their tactical approach through their own initiative if this should be found necessary during a game.

It is a happy circumstance that puts at the disposal of our national coach Helmut Schoen two such dominating players as Beckenbauer and Netzer. They are so outstanding that they alone are able to exert the decisive influence on a match. But perhaps even more important, the other players are far more than mere 'water-carriers' for these two great stars.

Each of the players brings his own ideas into play during matches and it is this homogeneous quality of the team that makes it so difficult to beat. Were this not so then it would be theoretically possible to stifle the German attack by close-marking Beckenbauer and Netzer. Anyone that attempted to concentrate on the two big stars would find Breitner, Muller, Hoeness, creating havoc in the spaces that were inevitably left. This is Germany's real strength – two quite outstanding stars but allied to a real

Karl-Heinz Heimann.

depth of talent that is without equal anywhere else in the world.

Yet despite this knowledge, I still hesitate.

We Germans have more cause than most to recall the World Cup of 1954 and it is this that makes me ultra-cautious about the World Cup. The memories still linger of that great Hungarian team spearheaded by Puskas, Kocsis, and Hidegkuti; speeding from victory to victory in the early fifties.

They even stormed the 'fortress' of Wembley by 6–3 and thrashed England 7–1 in the return a few months later. But they failed in the 1954 World Cup Final after more than 50 games without a single defeat and, more than that, after leading early in the Final by two goals to nil. There is no need to think of disasters like having Beckenbauer or Netzer injured. It is enough to remember the fate of the Hungarians in 1954 and the 'unbeatable' Brazilians of 1950.

Trying to name a challenger is somewhat difficult right now. Looking around Europe the traditional super-powers offer a somewhat disappointing sight. What is being shown by Sir Alf Ramsey's **ENGLAND** team seems to be only sterile workmanship without a spark of spirit. Moreover there is no outstanding individual like a Bobby Charlton to contribute the unexpected.

ITALY, meanwhile, have shown at national level that they are now willing, perhaps even eager, to give up their stubborn *catenaccio*. Though they now want to play attacking football they haven't yet learned how to do it. As for **RUSSIA**, they don't even have a light to guide them. They are in desperate need of a system as well as a style and more than that they don't yet even seem to have any conception of where they want to go.

With **HUNGARY** it seems to be much the same, and the **YUGOSLAVS** appear to have lost their will to struggle. Most teams are greatly in need of strong personalities. Real stars who can decide the result of matches single-handed and can be a prop for their colleagues.

Events may prove me wrong, but I was very impressed last year by **POLAND** when they played here in Munich in the Olympic Games. Their victory was a just reward for a clear-cut decision to opt for constructive football. Moreover, they possess players with powerful personalities in Lubanski and Szoltysik. They represent a real barrier on England's route to the final stages.

Elsewhere, the only possible challengers will come from South America and pride of place here must go to Brazil. **ARGENTINA** and **URUGUAY** have been, and still are, suffering from the effects of a severe financial crisis that has afflicted their football. **PERU** has the talent to do well but it would be quite incredible if they created a real surprise, for they have still to find an adequate replacement for their manager of 1970: Didi.

So we come back again to Brazil. No other country has prepared its path so steadily or with such care and precision. The experience of Mexico in 1970 has proven that it is worthwhile to organise the preparations thoroughly. Each World Cup of recent years has created the conditions in which the game has developed for the following period. After 1958 the technique of Brazil's stars and their 4-2-4 tactics conquered the entire world. But after 1962 and still worse after 1966 the game went entirely negative. Football all but disappeared and playing was replaced by fighting.

Since Mexico and 1970 the game has changed in many aspects. The much dreaded heat and altitude which prevailed forced everyone to preserve their physical strength and make greater use of technical and tactical weapons. How fruitful this experience

Zygfryd Szoltysik, of Gornik Zabrze and Poland . . . 'Player with a powerful personality'.

was has been demonstrated by the German team. It learned its lesson in Mexico and it has not forgotten it.

The change from speed-play to a game with frequently varying rhythm and greater technical skill was adopted first under the stress of the climatic conditions in Mexico. But today this new style is maintained intentionally and has led directly to successes that no one would have expected from German football.

It would be truly wonderful if this new game could find followers and quite apart from the result of the final I would be delighted if it were said after the next World Cup:

> *'It has given a clear lead to modern football and set an example for a new conception of the game. It has proved that beautiful football can also be successful football.'*

39

SPAIN MAY OPEN DOORS AGAIN TO WORLD STARS

DURING the time that I have played for Real Madrid, football in Spain has not really become more violent or dirty, but it is fairly violent, and sometimes I feel the game as a whole has been damaged. There is a continuing tendancy for more aggression, and violence threatens the very existence of the game as we know it now.

BY MANUEL VELAZQUEZ
Real Madrid and Spain

Spanish football is not the *most* violent or aggressive, and in my experience the toughest team I've played against was Standard Liege of Belgium, who put us out of the European Cup.

Violence and aggression are among the biggest problems facing the game today, and I'm sure that fully professional referees would do much to improve matters. At the moment in Spain, referees receive only 8,000 pesetas for controlling a First Division game, around £50; which is more than officials get in many countries but still not enough, I think. Full-time referees could go a long way to solving many of the problems which now face the game.

It has been suggested that perhaps foreign referees could be imported, but in my view this is not necessary, and would be too extreme a measure. Make the referees full-time, and the authorities could become more selective.

Another important question concerns the importation of foreign players, which enabled Spanish football to reach a peak in the 1950's that has not since been matched. For many years now, only players of proven Spanish descent have been allowed in Spain and the result is that too many mediocre players are being signed for excessive fees because the supply does not match the demand.

This, I believe, is a critical point for the Spanish game though, of course, there is no guarantee that the world's top players would be attracted to Spain. Nevertheless, if it were allowed, an influx of foreign talent could only do good, and there are

many outstanding players that might be persuaded here. Not long ago we met an outstanding individual, Nicolae Dobrin, who played against us in a European Cup game for the Rumanian side Argesul Pitesti. He is an admirable technical player, though inclined to be something of an individualist. Largely unknown, he indicates the

depth of talent available if the Spanish frontiers were opened to foreigners once more.

If the rules are changed to allow foreigners here it seems likely that the numbers would be limited. The most commonly-quoted figure is two per club though I think this is too little. To provide real competition for places the number could be higher, and some of the players I would like to see playing for Real Madrid include Dragan Dzajic (Yugoslavia), Johan Cruyff (Holland), Gunter Netzer (West Germany), and his countryman, Gerd Muller. They would fetch a small fortune in transfer fees but the arrival of such players would transform Real Madrid, and Spanish football generally.

The best Real team I have played in was that which won the European Cup in 1966, when we beat Partizan Belgrade in the final 2–1. That side included several players of vast experience and was altogether more formidable than the team that won the Championship for Real in 1971–72. The present team is younger, and lacking in the vital ingredient, experience; though some of them are very good indeed.

Perhaps the strongest team Real have had since then was the side that won the Championship in 1968–69. In that year we set an all-time Spanish record by being beaten only once in the entire League programme. The key men then were all experienced campaigners, including Sanchis, Pirri, Zoco, Amancio, and Gento. But there can be no

Two brilliant shots from Derby County's European Cup-tie against Zeljeznicar. (Left) It's John O'Hare forcing a great save from 'keeper Janjus. (Right) It's O'Hare again, man in the middle in a grouping that could almost be a charade for a 'Panto Horse'.

doubt that the quality of Real's play has declined since the early 1960's and I don't think anyone would deny it.

This decline was inevitable with the passing of great players like Ferenc Puskas and Alfredo Di Stefano, and there has been no chance to replace them with others of comparable ability. I never had the pleasure of playing with Di Stefano, though I did play a few games with Puskas. What a player he was. I had the formidable, even impossible, task of replacing him in the Real side.

Among the teams of today, I think the English are very strong. I have played for Real against two very formidable English clubs, Chelsea and Manchester United. Though the last named is going through a difficult time now they were a very good side indeed two or three years ago.

I have always admired the English game, which at its best has something like the right balance between ability and physical qualities. But today it is the West Germans who lead the way. With players like Netzer, Beckenbauer, and Muller they set the pattern of the future for everyone. To match them, it is necessary to find the outstanding individual players who can blend their talents for the good of the team as a whole. That is not so easy.

Karol Dobias with his wife.

CZECHS GIVE EU
'SMALL TOWN N

By KAROL DOBIAS

Czechoslovakia's Footballer
of the Year 1970 and
1971; right back of
Spartak Trnava

(Bottom left) Karol Dobias (on left), in Trnava colours, forces past Stratil of Teplice in a Czech League game. (Right) Dobias (dark shirt) is tackled by East Germany's Hans-Jurgen Kreische in an international match in Berlin.

WE didn't qualify for the 1966 World Cup and Scotland failed to get there when I played in Mexico for Czechoslovakia four years later. So my first opportunity to see them came in last year's 'Mini-World Cup', the Brazilian Independence Cup. My impression then was not a good one, though we didn't play well against Scotland ourselves. The result, o–o, indicates it was a poor game.

As I recall, the Czech team tried hard enough but it was one of our off-days. I remember, clearly, forming the impression that the Scottish players were not very interested. It seemed to me that they were in Brazil in a holiday mood rather than for serious football.

Later, I saw on television extracts from Scotland's two World Cup qualifying games with Denmark. It was obvious right away that there is a different approach now. I recognised eight of the players that we played against in Brazil; but they played quite differently, and with much more enthusiasm and determination.

My opinion is that we are going to have a real struggle to qualify for the World Cup. It will be wide open until the final whistle in our two matches and could go either way. Obviously, there is a new mood in the Scottish camp.

I had heard that Scottish players didn't like playing for the national team, preferring to play for their clubs; but if this were ever true it has clearly changed. Our manager, Mr. Vaclav Jezek, saw Scotland against Denmark and he confirmed this. He said before one of our friendly games last autumn that a new national enthusiasm has awakened in Scotland.

From what I saw against Denmark, the Scottish players are really professional in their approach to the game and they are all good fighters. I say that in the best sense. Not that they want to fight, but that they don't give up. They looked to me to be particularly strong in one-against-one duels, and they use the strength of their bodies well. I think, also, they are generally stronger at heading the ball than we are in Czechoslovakia and they certainly

45

do a lot of good running off the ball in support of each other. They play good modern football, and they play it hard.

In Czechoslovakia there is a lack of this fighting ability or enthusiasm, 'will to win', or whatever you want to call it. There is also a big weakness in our lack of physical powers, strength, stamina, and much less willingness to run. We play what I call 'comfortable' football. For example if we are winning 1–0 or 2–0 we relax, satisfied with what we have achieved, and prefer to hold on to our lead rather than press our advantage and build up a bigger score.

Our most important players are my Trnava colleagues Adamec, Hagara, Kuna, and the Dukla goalkeeper Ivo Viktor. There has been some controversy about Adamec and Viktor here in Czechoslovakia. Personally I would always prefer to have them in the side.

Ivo Viktor of Dukla and Czechoslovakia . . . 'Always prefer to have him in the side'.

Adamec used to be a regular scorer but he is 32 now and not so quick. He still has a tremendous shot but now he plays in midfield, where he does a lot of good work. Though slower, he has a tremendous football intelligence. Hagara who plays stopper was converted from left back and he is not only very difficult to beat but is also a real organiser, always talking – calling advice and making sure no one sneaks into the danger area without being picked up by a defender. Kuna is a great player, too, though he has been out of action a lot this season with injuries.

In my opinion there are two quite different games of football being played in Czechoslovakia today, and this is one of our biggest problems. The old traditional leaders of the Czech game are Sparta and Slavia in Prague, but they have fallen back badly in recent years. They still play the old-fashioned slow, short-passing, game.

Sparta are quite a lot better than Slavia, thanks to their fighting spirit, especially in front of their own crowd. But like Slavia their build up from defence to attack is much too slow, often playing sideways and sometimes backwards towards their own goal. There are some good individual players in the Prague clubs but they play too slowly and too much as individuals.

Anton Malatinsky, Trnava's coach . . . 'He has friends everywhere'. (Right) Dobias scores from a penalty kick for Czechoslovakia against Luxembourg 'keeper Moes.

At Trnava we play the new game, thanks to our coach Anton Malatinsky. There is also a different attitude towards the game in Slovakia as compared with Prague. Here in Slovakia even the smallest village has its own football ground and, seven days a week, the grounds are crowded with youngsters playing all day. I know there are small villages near Prague but somehow their way of living has changed.

In Slovakia football is a way of life and as a result the players with senior clubs have a better morale, more discipline, and are also more ambitious. The big clubs in Slovakia have a much bigger choice when it comes to signing new young players, and this is specially true at Trnava. Thanks to Mr. Malatinsky we have won the Championship four times in five years. Now every boy in Slovakia dreams of playing for Spartak Trnava.

Mr. Malatinsky has friends everywhere. They write or phone to tell him whenever they see a boy with real ability. He spends a lot of his free time checking on recommended youngsters. To a lesser extent, this is also true of other Slovak clubs such as Presov, Zilina, and Nitra.

What Spartak Trnava have done is a real achievement for a town with a total population of only 40,000. In 1969, after we had won the Championship for the first time, we reached the semi-final of the European Cup. For a small-town team that was almost a miracle. As it was, we lost only 3–2 on aggregate to Ajax Amsterdam . . . and we could have beaten them.

In Holland we lost 3–0, but all the goals came from defensive errors. At home, when we were leading 2–0, Adamec was through on his own and missed a great chance. We are more experienced

now, but so, too, are Ajax. That was our greatest achievement, I think; but I also feel our present team is even better, and we could with a little bit of luck bring off a real surprise.

One of our biggest handicaps is a lack of international experience. Apart from our European Cup games we very rarely have the time or the opportunity to play against the best sides in other countries. Everyone here at Trnava is really ambitious and believes in the club. Our training is modern, too, in that it is related to the needs of the game.

Every training session we have is different, with everyone working hard. We go through different

We've played so much football for the last five years and I seem to be going through a bad spell. The truth is that I probably need a rest from the game. The others must feel the strain, too. Almost every week we play on Saturday or Sunday and again on Wednesday. This last year I have suffered from old injuries that linger on. There is not time to rest and settle these old knocks. Quite often the Club doctor has to give me pain-killing injections before each game.

Almost everyone at Trnava is a local product. All the players were born in the villages in the neighbourhood or, like myself, Fandel, and Varadin, were actually born in the town. When I was five my

Jozef Adamec . . . 'tremendous football intelligence'.

Ladislav Kuna . . . 'out a lot with injuries'.

Vladimir Hagara . . . 'real organiser, always talking'.

passing combinations; say the right-back, right-half, and right-winger in a small group first alone, and then against defenders. The variations are countless but thanks to Mr. Malatinsky, who knows a great deal about football, and will not keep a player unless he works hard and is enthusiastic, we have a high morale.

We don't have too much time to waste if we are going to achieve something big. The players are mostly in their late twenties now, and we lack top-level experience. For example, we have never yet played against an Italian club in my time. Adamec, Hagara, and Kabat are our oldest players. Though I am 26 now and comparatively young, I have problems, too.

parents moved a few miles to an even smaller town Handlova, but when I was 15 we moved back to Trnava. I played in schoolboy football in Handlova and joined the Spartak Trnava Youth team when I was 15.

Three years later Mr. Malatinsky invited me to join the senior squad. I think this is a big part of Spartak Trnava's success. Local boys know the club is willing to give good, skilful, youngsters their chance, and the present team is exclusively local born, to prove it. That, and the hard work, understanding, and confidence of Mr. Malatinsky has brought the Club success. And it's all been done without even one big transfer.

Utter concentration, and a real competitor . . . Chelsea's David Webb (right) measures this one away carefully from the back of West Ham's Trevor Brooking.

WHY IS I
SO LONG

PUZZLE: If Cyprus can beat an old-established footballing country like Northern Ireland which has the benefit of calling on English club players, why is it that a mighty nation like the United States of America is taking such an unconscionable time to establish Soccer on an international scale?

The immediate reaction might be to reply that the United States beat England in the World Cup as long ago as 1950. But that was possibly the most surprising result in the history of Association Football and is almost impossible to account for, especially when the England team read like this (though I have no desire to embarrass Sir Alf Ramsey and the other famous men in the team):

Williams (Wolverhampton Wanderers); Ramsey (Tottenham Hotspur), Aston (Manchester United) Wright (Wolverhampton Wanderers), Hughe (Liverpool), Dickinson (Portsmouth); Finney (Preston North End), Mannion (Middlesbrough), Bentley (Chelsea), Mortensen (Blackpool), Muller (Wolverhampton Wanderers).

There is, of course, no single reason for the failure of the United States to have since become a Soccer nation, though better propaganda for the game could not have been found than that astonishing defeat of England, the country which invented the game.

'Hear no evil, speak no evil' – is Manchester United' Willie Morgan (left) handing such a hint to Arsenal' Peter Storey? (Right) Denis Law (read Charlie George' praises, page 55) hustles Arsenal's Jeff Blockley and th sliding Bob McNab.

...AKING
AMERICA?

BY SIR MATT BUSBY

For a country to become a Soccer nation, the small boys of that nation, from, say, four years old, have to be given a big round ball for Christmas and to be encouraged to kick it. Instinctively those who are going to be good players will kick it as a Soccer ball should be kicked.

They may not have all the attributes of a footballer and it is most unlikely that more than a small minority of them will have all the attributes, even in embryo, of a professional footballer of the future.

But they will have had a chance to find out, in the only way possible to find out, by having a kick at a round ball, instead of having been given a small ball to throw and a bat to hit it with, which is what the vast majority of American boys have as presents for Christmas; or perhaps an oval one to throw about or kick as well as its eccentricity will allow.

Soon, then, the boys of six will be seen to be forming groups and evolving as teams, and playing the game in every spare moment. Small boys in Soccer

countries do an immense amount of training with a ball. In my day as a small boy we were sometimes lucky to be able to afford a ball of any description. So we kicked anything that could be made to act as one. Perhaps tightly-packed paper, or even an old tin can. But old tin cans were not much good for heading practice.

It is very rare that a teenager who has never played with a spherical football as an infant will suddenly discover that he is a Soccer player in the making.

On the other hand there must be many American boys who have never even seen a spherical football whose instincts, had they been encouraged, would have led them into the game at the highest standard. We shall never know, except that logic suggests that great footballers are born, not made, and that there is an equal percentage of boys with the gift for the game in any country.

The thing is that if boys are not encouraged to play almost from the cradle they are unlikely to play Soccer. And they are unlikely to be encouraged to play it unless all the boys in the neighbourhood are encouraged to do the same. In America the boys do the same with baseballs and oval footballs.

It is another fact of football life that Soccer is basically a working-class game, both from the playing and spectator viewpoint. I know that some players have degrees and that some spectators are doctors, and so on, but most are from the artisan section.

It is a fact of football life that non-affluent countries, since they do not provide so many rival interests like television, sophisticated toys, and the like, for small boys, and which also do not occupy so much time studying for General Certificates of Education, are better training grounds for the young in a game that is cheap. One ball is enough for 22 boys to kick to their hearts' content all day and every day. Hence the ball-control of some infants in, say, the South American countries, is quite prodigious.

The Britain of the depressing 'twenties and 'thirties was similar. As young boys, we would play three matches a day when we could; morning, afternoon, and night. Britain still provides plenty of footballers, because Britain was off to a good start, having played the game for more than a hundred years.

Colin Jackson of Rangers politely offers his back as a trampoline for scissoring Kilmarnock goal-hero Eddie Morrison (left). (Right) The mighty Scot from whom Manchester United are expecting so much – Lou Macari.

Nevertheless, I am not sure that Britain has not been left a little way behind by less affluent countries in the matter of ball control. We bow to no country for physical fitness or for courage, but I sometimes envy others their wizardry with the ball.

The point is, of course, that in America there have not yet sprung up enough areas wherein a Soccer ball is kicked by small boys from nursery days, and America is the affluent nation.

Because America is so affluent it has spent money

in abundance – or those interested in our game have – in trying to establish it. Many of our players have been over there, playing and coaching, and doubtless some are there still. Our top clubs have played exhibition matches there to show the Soccer flag. United States Football Association President Jim Maguire and his aides have worked tremendously hard on Soccer's behalf.

But a Soccer nation cannot be made out of dollars, not even the biggest pile of dollars imaginable. American Soccer people could persuade hundreds of our best players to go over there and play for their teams for huge wages, and the United States would be as far away as ever unless the whole thing started from the nurseries of every state.

Since Americans represent every country in Europe and since every country in Europe plays Soccer on an international scale, genetically there are many potential world-class players there.

While baseball and their own brand of football have such a grip, the genes of which will be different from Soccer genes, that potential might never be realised. But be sure that my requirements for the game to begin in the nursery will always be there.

You don't learn this game. You grow up with it.

DENIS LAW: 'UNIQUE, ARROGANT —HE LEFT ME BREATHLESS'

By CHARLIE GEORGE
Arsenal and England Under-23

I have many vivid memories of the days when I jostled through the turnstiles to endure the agony of an Arsenal defeat and surged out again to drown my sorrows in plastic-mug tea and to munch a hot-dog.

They are as important to me as later memories of my own Highbury battles. They remind me of images and old friends, and of a life before I pulled on an Arsenal shirt – days when I could enjoy the dream of a Highbury career.

In school-break times, in football matches that thundered with all the agony and intensity of Arsenal versus Tottenham, I saw myself as Denis Law, the only footballer ever to influence or impress me as a player.

For me, he was always the 'complete' footballer. And it was not just a question of ability. He had a unique style, a tremendous arrogance born out of a wonderful talent, and a confident authority that would leave me breathless with admiration.

Frank McLintock, Arsenal's supreme player, has that same authority but, with him, it's part of that gritty determination which drives him on towards success. He has shown that side of his character by maintaining his own high standards and driving the rest of us on to meet them.

Screened and covered, a near-perfect bit of goalkeeping from Hearts' Kenny Garland, who leaves no scope for Rangers' forward Derek Parlane. (Right) Charlie George with F.A. Cup – a 'King' at Highbury, though having to fight off a certain Republican feeling from time to time . . .

When George Male, former Arsenal full-back, asked me to train twice weekly at Billy Wright's Highbury in 1965, when I was still a schoolboy, I was stunned. But in May, 1966, when I signed apprentice forms, I'd grown used to the idea that the impossible dream was not perhaps so impossible after all.

The discipline required of a trainee footballer wa

a new experience – the muscle-tearing effort, th sweat, the worry of the ever-present fear of failure But then, in 1968, when I signed professional forms it had all been worth it.

When I recall the hard work of it all, and look back on those nights in the rain, I remember with special relish my Cup-winning goal against Liver pool in 1971. I felt elated watching the ball sneaking inside the post and seeing Ray Clemence stretching hopelessly for it.

There are times when a player hits a ball and knows on the moment of impact that it's a goal That Wembley shot was one like that. The specia flavour of that goal was that it answered Bil Shankly's 'Southern Softies' gibe. There's no club in the Football League for which I have any specia

(Left) one of Highbury's stalwarts, the wholehearted George Armstrong, here gritting his way through a tussle with Stoke's Mike Pejic. (Top) Liverpool manager Bill Shankly . . . 'Southern Softies' gibe was settled by George goal. (Right) Charlie George deep in the Arsenal goal-mouth, behind Jeff Blockley . . . helping out against Coventry's Roy Barry and Bobby Parker.

regard; neither is there one that I would dismiss . . . whether from the north or the south.

The F.A. Cup Final of 1971 when Arsenal clinched the 'double' is certainly the most treasured memory of my football album. One thing I remember particularly is the way the fantastic Liverpool crowd cheered us to the echo. You would have thought Liverpool had won! The Kop is surely the finest crowd in Britain . . . them and the Manchester United 'Stretford Enders'.

It's a memory to which I cling. Another is my first appearance in an England shirt with the Under-23 side last year. It gave me an appetite for international football that I hope to satisfy at Munich.

The World Cup is not the only Trophy of which I think. I want to see Arsenal win the European Cup,

too. Our first attempt was disappointing but we learned something, even if it was only that Ajax are a good side.

The Dutch side are certainly the best I've played against, including Benfica. They have players of tremendous skill and artistry and yet they are still physical enough to cope with hard, physical opposition. They have great flair in attack and depth in defence.

I'm often asked about my future. It's something I've never really thought about. I'm trusting that I will earn enough money from football to go into business after hanging up my boots. What business? I've no idea. I'm too involved with Arsenal and football to think too much about the future. It will have to take care of itself.

I still have the enthusiasm for football that I had during those schoolboy kickabouts. People are amazed when I tell them that I have no hobbies or interests outside the game. But why? Football is my hobby! In my book, that makes me lucky.

I don't care where I play. When I'm asked if I have a preference for playing in midfield or being a striker, I always say: 'No, I'm just happy to be playing'.

All footballers go their different ways when it's all over, and I'll go mine. One thing's certain, though. One day I'll be back on the North Bank and life will have turned full circle. Only the memories will have increased.

A wet collar will still be a wet collar.

Brought in as a substitute (top), Charlie George turned a 0–2 deficit against Newcastle into a 2–2 draw. But oh! that famous temper; here he seems to be making a grab at David Craig's throat. (Right) Two tough little men who epitomise the skill and determination that makes football giants – Arsenal's Alan Ball and Billy Bremner of Leeds.

SUDDENLY WINGERS ARE 'IN' AGAIN

BY PETER LORIMER

Leeds and Scotland

THERE was a time two or three years ago when wingers seemed to be out of fashion. Thinking then ran along the lines of 4-4-2 with two big fellows up the middle, but it didn't last long. Quite quickly, within the professional game, it was realised that concentrating one's attack up the centre made it too easy for the opposing defenders. Blocking the middle was easy; and so the emphasis switched again to wing play.

With at least one winger the attack has greater width. We at Leeds have two wingers, though for lengthy spells we've felt the lack of penetration on the left, having to do without the services of the injured Eddie Gray. With me on the right and Eddie on the left our attack is better balanced, and far more effective.

This is not to say that I play exclusively out on the right, though there is no reason why a Matthews'-type winger shouldn't do so. It's just that I prefer to be involved with the game and I have an understanding with our manager, Mr. Don Revie, that if I get bogged down on the right I can either drop deeper looking for the ball, or wander across the line of attack seeking chances to break through and shoot.

This greater width given back to attacking teams by the return of wingers is now almost universally accepted. All the top teams have penetrative players out wide on the flanks. For myself I can only say that I love going forward and there's nothing I like better than scoring goals. If I find I'm not getting shooting chances ploughing a furrow up and down the right, then I move.

I've been at Leeds since I was fifteen and for almost as long as I can remember the Club has always been handily placed for the final sprint to the honours at the end of the season. This, I think,

Peter Lorimer (above) . . . and if he looks unfamiliar, it's because he had to step in as deputy goalkeeper after Harvey's injury at Chelsea last season. (Right) Tough goal-line moment for Leicester 'keeper Peter Shilton – Lorimer is goal-side of him, but a lucky bounce ends the danger.

is a question of attitude and application. If you really believe in yourselves as we do at Leeds then it's taken for granted that you are going to be among the honours every year. This develops an acceptance of the 'Three Cup Finals a week' mentality which is so vital if a club is to be successful in our crowded fixture lists of today.

This Cup Final atmosphere is maintained at Leeds by our manager, whose most repeated phrase is 'If we win this one we'll win the League'. Mr. Revie says this every week, every game, and though it's been said so many times before it has real meaning. I believe that the mentality which comes from acceptance of this belief breeds success.

Of course other clubs have this will to do well, though in varying degrees. Liverpool are the most difficult side to beat any time, anywhere; a strong all-round side. We have the greatest respect for each other and always have well-fought, tightly-balanced matches with them.

Another side I have felt to be on the verge of really doing something for some time is Chelsea. Every year I look on them as a danger, a potential Championship contender. Yet somehow, despite many good performances, they never seem to be there at the end. Chelsea, perhaps, are the kind of team to back in the Cup competitions. Capable of beating anyone on their day, but finding it difficult

to concentrate over lengthy periods.

What's missing at some of the good other clubs is maybe something of Mr. Revie's 'If we win this one . . .'.

It's misleading to mention just two other clubs. This suggests there is little competition, and it just isn't true. The English League is the most difficult Competition in the world to win, demanding maximum effort every week over endless months. Every game is like a Cup Final when you have your sights set on the Championship. You just can't afford to be beaten more than three or four times if you are to be in there at the end.

If you're at the top, setting the pace, then the pressure is even greater. Everyone you play wants to beat you. I think Leeds United have earned the kind of reputation that helps build an 'atmosphere'

wherever we play these days. Almost everyone is capable of raising their game for the day. In London, for example, it's always difficult to get a result.

But today, the League and Cup programme is added to by the international fixtures that seem to follow endlessly every year nowadays. I'm not complaining about being included in Scotland's squad. I'm highly delighted every time the squad is named and I see my own name among them. But I do have some difficulties getting keyed-up for friendly matches at the end of a long hard season at home.

World Cup games and the Brazilian tournament staged last year are always exciting for everyone involved. With the attitude developed at Leeds it's no problem maintaining the necessary right attitude towards competitive games. Even though it cuts down the off-season break, which seems to get smaller each year.

But I just cannot whip up enthusiasm for friendlies. I don't think the fans like them either. There's nothing at stake, no atmosphere, and the crowds seem to underline this. They are often very poor for friendly internationals.

The World Cup is another matter, and I'm sure Scotland are going to do well this time. I didn't play against Czechoslovakia last year in Brazil but Billy Bremner did and he told me a lot about them. The Czechs are our only obstacle in the World Cup now, our having beaten Denmark twice. Billy told me the Czechs are no more than an average side.

We have a really good spirit in the Scottish squad and I fancy our chances if we meet England during the final stages in Germany. At one time I thought England might have trouble qualifying, but after they beat Wales in Cardiff I changed my opinion. In fact it could be that Wales will help England, for though they lost their chance of qualifying when they lost at home to England, they still look capable to me of beating Poland at home. That of course would help make things easier for England.

It should be a really great World Cup, and I'm looking forward to it – assuming I manage to keep my place. The new Scottish team is just developing and by the time the final stages come round I feel we'll have a great chance to really do something.

Don Revie (with Billy Bremner, top) – 'Every week a Cup Final'. (Left) Joe Royle of Everton looks every inch an England leader as he climbs to put a header past Leeds' Jackie Charlton. (Right) Roy McFarland of Derby (left) just gets the edge this time on Leeds' Eddie Gray : 'With me on the right and Eddie on the left our attack . . . is far more effective'.

TOO MANY GAMES? — NO, SIR!

By STEVE PERRYMAN
of Tottenham Hotspur

THERE'S been a lot of talk about fixture congestion and too much football being bad for the game. Speaking for myself, I enjoy being involved in European competitions as well as our domestic football. The pressures on fixtures would have been relieved if we had been knocked-out in the early rounds of the Football League Cup or the UEFA Cup; but that would have meant that we were not being successful. So if fixture pile-ups and success go together I'd always prefer to be successful.

I'm still only 21 and it may be that when I'm around 27 or 28 I might feel a bit differently; but I hope not. I enjoy playing, I love to travel, and I think that your play as a team improves through playing together more often. The more you play together, the easier it becomes to read each other's minds and anticipate things in matches. Looking at things all round, I wouldn't want a change.

However, I would not advocate a European Super-League. I think the balance is just right as it is now with the big three international competitions. In my opinion the British public likes to see

Rough moment for Spurs (top left) as Derby's John O'Hare looses a truly spectacular shot. (Below) Intelligent mover Martin Peters of Spurs glides round this tackle from West Ham's Tommy Taylor.

The E.U.F.A. Cup for Spurs, to be followed by the League Cup less than a year later. (Above) Martin Chivers scores Spurs' first against Wolves. (Below) Cyril Knowles tackles Wolves' Richards, helping out Pat Jennings. (Right) 'Gillie' – Spurs' veteran Alan Gilzean – always so good in the air, pips Liverpool's Chris Lawler to this one.

top-class Continental teams over here, but only in competitive games. If it became a regular thing, I think the novelty might begin to wear off and the interest of the fans would decline.

When you have mid-week matches, in addition to the usual League and Cup games at weekends, I find it a nice change from the usual routine of training between games. I look forward to travelling abroad and seeing new places. In a week when we go abroad for an away match we travel on Monday, do a little light training on Tuesday, play the game on Wednesday, and come home the next day.

Of course, we prepare specially for all our games, but, for example, half-way through last season we'd already played Liverpool three times. In these

situations both sides get to know each other's moves and learn how to counter them. But playing in Europe is different.

We players never get the chance to see our future opponents but of course our coach and manager do. They tell us all about them, their best players and style of play, their strengths and weaknesses, and we work with that particular opponent in mind in our training before we meet. So new opponents bring new challenges.

When we actually come to the game it's a new experience and there's always something new to learn. Perhaps the best example of this was provided by AC Milan, whom we met in the old Fairs Cup. They played with four defenders at the back and a spare man behind. That presented a new problem and you learn from it.

You never know, English clubs don't play with a free-back as yet but if we ever met one I'm sure we'd be better equipped to cope with the problems that presents because of our experiences in European competition.

AC Milan are probably the best side we've met abroad but the Yugoslavs, Red Star-Belgrade are also very good. Being a midfield player myself, I pay special attention to their midfield players and it seems to me that the best foreign sides always have one really outstanding player, and he is usually a creative midfield player. Gianni Rivera is one of these exceptionally gifted players; another is Jovan

Pat Jennings of Spurs (left); brilliant, experienced, one of Britain's finest goalkeepers. (Right) Derby's Roger Davies has Mike England and Kinnear of Spurs bowing and kneeling in this F.A. Cup-tie.

Sentimental moment for 46,000 Spurs' fans — former idol Jimmy Greaves, Martin Peters beside him, leads out the team for his benefit match against Holland's Feyenoord. (Right) Jovan Acimovic of Red Star and Yugoslavia . . . 'Plays the possession game really well'.

Acimovic of Red Star. He had two fine games against us.

We were warned before the game against Red Star that they were very good, and they were; though I think they played better against us in London than they did in Belgrade. In the first leg the onus was on us to score goals but before we could do that we had to get the ball. Against such skilful players as Acimovic, who can play the possession game really well, the big problem was to get the ball away from them.

In the end, the traditional British qualities of

fighting spirit, determination, and the ability to win the ball and score goals won out; but Red Star were very good. Acimovic was outstanding. He is tremendously skilful and a very good positional player. Above all, he screens the ball by using his body well. Getting the ball from him can be a real problem. The ball is there, and you go in for it. Suddenly it's gone and you find yourself hitting his body.

There are quite a few exotic places that I would yet like to visit – places like Jamaica and the Bahamas. I'd also like to tour Australia some time. When I was in the Spurs Youth teams I travelled to Belgium and Holland but my first real trip abroad was to the United States and Canada.

I hadn't played in the first team at that time and it was a real experience in every way. I think the appeal of the United States is its variety and its largeness. The most spectacular single thing I saw there was the Niagara Falls.

I hope to go on seeing such spectacular sights for a long time and that means, in the main, being successful in the English competitions in order to stay in Europe. If League football gives me my bread and butter then European competition provides the jam and the cream. I'm all for that.

DUSAN BAJEVIC (Velez and Yugoslavia) Tall, well made centre-forward, excellent in the air and no tyro on the ground. He was leading scorer in the Brazilian Independence Tournament played in the summer of 1972. Among his exploits were five out of ten goals against Venezuela and another two when his country beat Argentina in a fiery third place match in Rio. He also had a cool, impressive game against England at Wembley, the following October.

HORST BLANKENBURG (Ajax Amsterdam) This blond defender became, in season 1971/72, Ajax's attacking sweeper, or *libero*, with remarkable success. He has none of the graces and elegance of his compatriot Franz Beckenbauer, but he is a vigorous, enterprising player, and he does the job as well as Ajax want. He came to them from Munich 1860 at the end of 1970 on a two-year contract – he himself is German – and played as a substitute in their winning 1971 European Cup Final against Panathinaikos at Wembley. By the following Final, against Inter in Rotterdam, he was a prominent, established member of the Ajax side. A further honour came in January 1973, when he played again at Wembley, this time in the Fanfare for Europe match for the Six against the Three.

PAUL BREITNER (Bayern Munich and West Germany) A revelation of season 1971/72, which he consummated with a fine performance in the European Nations Cup Final for West Germany against Russia. He was still only 20, yet he took to international football like a duck to water, giving a particularly splendid performance of attacking, overlapping left-back play against England in the quarter-final, at Wembley in April, 1972. A product

of Bayern Munich, he is a serious young man, who intends to devote a portion of his earnings to a home for handicapped children. Born 3-9-51.

GIORGIO CHINAGLIA (Lazio and Italy) This 25-year-old centre-forward's story seems slightly too good to be true. Brought to Cardiff as a six-year-old from Massa in Tuscany – where the

The skill and determination which makes Steve Perryman such a fine prospect (left) also brings a gasp from Liverpool's Ian Callaghan. (Right) Serge Chiesa of Lyon and France ... 'great precocity and gifts'.

marble comes from – the son of a poor Italian immigrant, he played for Cardiff Boys, was signed by Swansea Town; and given a free transfer at 19. He did not get on with the Swansea manager; but no other club wanted him, either. Reluctantly he went back to Italy to play for his local, Third Division (Serie C) club, Massese. He there took wing, was signed by Internapoli (also in Serie C) for £65,000, then, after a couple of prolific seasons, by Lazio of Rome, for double the sum. In season 1971/72 he helped them to promotion from Serie B to Serie A, was capped for Italy and made nearly £75,000. Tall, well-built, with a fine right foot; but surprisingly modest in the air. Born 24-1-47.

SERGE CHIESA (Lyon and France) A little inside-forward of great precocity and gifts, which he has been curiously shy about fulfilling. Born in Casablanca, Morocco, on December 25, 1950, a Christmas baby, he played as an amateur for Montferrand, got into the French Youth team, and was so outstanding that he was concurrently picked for a full French international team; an almost unheard-of achievement. It came in 1969, at Beziers. Soon afterwards he won his first cap, proper, against Norway in a World Cup match in Oslo, retained his place for the following game, against Sweden, but lost his place the following season. It was only in October, 1972, that, recalled as a late choice against Russia, he brilliantly re-affirmed his talents as a ball-playing, creative inside-forward of international class. By now he was a mature League player with Lyon, who had beaten a host of contestants to his signature. Yet when the time came to play the next, World Cup qualifying, international, against Eire in Dublin, Chiesa refused. He was subject, he said, to home sickness. A puzzling, deeply shy and modest, player.

ELIAS FIGUEROA (Internacional Porto Alegre and Chile) This athletic Chilean is reckoned to be the best centre-half in Brazilian football; just as, prior to his arrival in Porto Alegre, he was thought one of the best in Uruguay. He played then for the famous Penarol club of Montevideo; who, mysteriously, wouldn't give him permission to represent Chile in the World Cup eliminators for 1970. Malign tongues had it that Penarol had orders from on high; that the officials of the

Paul Breitner . . . 'a revelation . . . and a serious young man'.

national team had too much fear and respect for his defensive abilities – for Uruguay and Chile were in the same group. Penarol, desperate for money, sold him to Internacional, where he was an immediate success. Tall and well-made, he is as formidable on the ground as in the air, and has a splendid touch for the ball. He says he loves playing in Brazil, where it's a pleasure to play in such skilful football, against such clever forwards.

ARCHIE GEMMILL (Derby County and Scotland) A key player in Derby County's League Championship success of 1971/72 and their subsequent fine run in the European Cup, Gemmill is a classic Scottish inside-forward; with one major qualification. Though the kind of tiny ball player Scotland has given us since the days of James, through Steel and Logie, he is electrically fast; like these last two, but unlike the traditional Scottish 'general'. If Gemmill has a fault, it is that he is inclined in his eagerness to 'carry' the ball, but he has great heart and keen, swift intelligence. Born in Paisley, he developed with the local club, St. Mirren, and was brought into English football by Preston North End. Brian Clough shrewdly bought him for Derby to take the place of another fine little inside-forward in Carlin. Played all three home internationals for Scotland in the 1972 tournament,

Uli Hoeness (left) . . . 'plays anywhere in attack'. (Above) Josef Heynckes . . . 'the ideal striker'.

Murtaz Khurtsilava . . . 'a great deal of moral courage'.

and has never been better than in the European Cup later that year against Zeljeznicar and, in the first half, Benfica. He has – unlike many a Scot – phenomenal self-control when maltreated; as he so often is, especially by foreign teams.

JOSEF HEYNCKES (Borussia Monchengladbach and West Germany) Centre-forward or winger, initially the first, Heynckes is in effect the

ideal striker, quite happy on the flanks or in the middle, and dangerous wherever he may be Characteristically, he was intimately involved with all three of West Germany's goals in the 1972 Nations Cup Final against Russia; even though he got none of them himself. It was after his shot had been blocked that Muller scored the first, his splendid through pass made the second, and he exchanged passes with Schwarzenbeck to make Muller the third. He forced his way into that excellent team after substituting young Hoeness in Berlin against England; the return quarter-final. After that, he was impossible to keep out. He is quick, direct, intelligent and a fine finisher. First capped for West Germany as a centre-forward helped Borussia to two consecutive League Championships in 1970 and 1971.

ULI HOENESS (Bayern Munich and West Germany) Blond inside-forward who made his debut for West Germany against England at Wembley in April, 1972, a Nations Cup quarter-final, at 20, and played brilliantly; mostly on the left wing. In fact he can play anywhere in attack, and does; either in midfield or in the striking positions. He is fast, brave, very penetrative; even if he did inevitably look a little tired by the time it came to playing for his country in the Nations Cup Finals, when he helped them to win the title in

Jordao . . . 'compared with the celebrated Eusebio'.

Belgium. Having carefully stayed amateur, he was then able to represent the West German Olympic soccer team, in Munich. A player with an impressive present and a dazzling future. Born 5-1-52.

JORDAO (Benfica and Portugal) One of three 18-year-old players found by Benfica in Angola, Jordao broke through emphatically in 1972 while still only 19 years old; he was in fact born in Benguela on August 9, 1952. His long, slender legs make him skimming down the left wing with splendid, spectacular effect, but he himself prefers to play in midfield or at centre-forward. In fact he led the Benfica attack on their 1971/72 tour of Brazil with tremendous success; returning there a few months later as a member of the Portuguese international team which reached the Final of the Independence Cup. A wonderfully exciting, exhil-

The handsome Leivinha, 'One of Brazil's major hopes for the World Cup'. (Above) In the one-goal defeat of Portugal, Leivinha shows what a goalmouth danger he can be, watched (left) by the great Tostao.

Joe Royle takes a flying dive to go near against Yugoslav 'keeper Maric at Wembley . . . 'Like Dean and Lawton he is formidable in the air'. (Right) Chelsea's Ian Hutchinson (No. 10) beaten in the air by Derby's Colin Todd: 'Todd is to all appearances the model professional'.

arating player who has been compared with the celebrated Eusebio; and who combines with him splendidly.

MURTAS KHURTSILAVA (Dynamo Tbilisi and Russia) It takes a great deal of moral courage and ability to look outstanding in a European Nations Cup Final in which your team is being thrashed, 3–0; but the muscular Khurtsilava managed it, for Russia against West Germany in the 1972 Brussels match. Not only did he resist splendidly at centre-half, he even trundled upfield twice for splendid shots at goal, one of which hit the bar. Born on January 1, 1943, he can play as stopper or sweeper, and represented his country in the World Cup final stages of 1966 and 1970. He succeeded Chesternijev as captain in season 1971/72. Dark and almost squat, he looked the Georgian that he is; a defender of great resilience and power.

LEIVINHA (Palmeiras and Brazil) I have admired this admirably gifted, striking inside-forward since, five years ago, I saw him score a memorable individual goal for Portuguese Desportes against Fiorentina, in a friendly match in Florence. Blond and well built, he casually left man after man behind, in the best Brazilian style. His *nom de guerre* as 'Leivinha' refers, in fact, to his earlier days, when he was slender and a lightweight. Palmeiras bought him from Portuguesa and in 1972 he was capped by Brazil in the Independence Tournament, playing centre-forward in the Final against Portugal, though substituted by Dario. One of Brazil's major hopes for the World Cup of 1974.

ROY McFARLAND (Derby County and England) A centre-half who steadily and solidly established himself as England's first choice, after helping Derby County to win the Second Division Championship; following which, he helped them materially to win the First. Liverpool-born, McFarland was one who got away . . . from the two great Liverpudlian clubs. In fact it was Tranmere Rovers who signed him, and Brian Clough who made a foray in the night to buy him for Derby County. It may be true that McFarland is better on the ground than in the air, but he still heads some splendid, vital goals from free kicks and corners. He is a

Herbert Wimmer . . . 'Perfectly suited to total football'.

tough, resourceful, sometimes unceremonious player, first capped by England in 1970/71.

OMAR PASTORIZA (Monaco and Argentina)

It was ironic, indeed, that only weeks after playing for Independiente of Buenos Aires as their captain and midfield orchestrator, in the Intercontinental Championship, Pastoriza should be diverted into the pleasant backwaters of French Second Division football, with Monaco. It was an anticlimactic end to a turbulent 1972 for this gifted, thoughtful, but sometimes violent player; captain of country as well as club, a fine header of the ball, if somewhat lacking in pace. He had earlier been chosen South American Footballer of the Year, was skipper of the Argentinian team which reached the third place match in the Brazilian Independence Cup; a heated occasion on which Pastoriza himself was sent off. Stefan Kovacs, the Ajax manager, however, praised his sportsmanship in the turbulent first leg of the World Club Championship. And so to Monaco, crowds of 2,000 a time; and, ironically, more money than he could find in Argentina, where enthusiasm reaches boiling point.

JOE ROYLE (Everton and England)

A centre-forward well in the tradition of Dixie Dean and Tommy Lawton, his predecessors at Everton; like them, he is formidable in the air. It was sad that almost immediately after a splendid display for an otherwise mediocre England against Yugoslavia, at Wembley, in October, 1972. Royle should be forced to drop out of the game for months, with an injury. A Liverpudlian, developed at Goodison, he had won his first cap in 1970, against Malta, in Valetta. After that, his career seemed to have gone into a passing decline; until his splendid, vigorous performance against Yugoslavia.

GEORG SCHWARZENBECK (Bayern Munich and West Germany)

A centre-half ideally suited to the pattern of 'total football', always ready and eager to break upfield; as he did with signal success in the Final of the 1972 European Nations Cup, to make his team's third goal against Russia. He was still only 24 and previously, in the quarter-final, had confidently played Martin Chivers out of the game both at Wembley and in Berlin. Bayern signed him from the local Munich club Sportfreund, in 1966. Born 3-8-48.

PEPE SANTORO (Independiente and Argentina)

That good goalkeepers improve with the years was shown in 1972 by Santoro, the dark handsome, elegant Independiente 'keeper. He played a major part in his team's success in the Copa de los Libertadores, the South American Cup, not least in the Final when he had to make a limited but essential number of saves against the Peruvians Universitario. This was especially pleasing to the Argentinian fans and Press, as it was nine years since Independiente had last won the Libertadores Cup; and on that occasion too, against Nacional Santoro had played a vital part. He went on, in 1972, to play against Ajax in the Intercontinental Cup, to regain his place as the Argentinian international goalkeeper, and to appear for the South American representative team against Europe at Basle, in October. He is particularly good at timing his rushes from goal and beyond the area, when a forward breaks through.

COLIN TODD (Derby County and England)

When Colin Todd was suspended for two years from international football for crying off the Under-23 tour of Eastern Europe in the summer of

1972, it seemed a classic case of cutting off one's nose to spite one's face. Quiet, modest and dedicated, Todd is to all appearances the model professional; and the obvious, eventual successor to Bobby Moore in the England back four. Derby County paid £170,000 for him to Sunderland and have not regretted a penny of it; he helped them to win the First Division title in 1972, dovetailed beautifully with Roy McFarland as a second stopper, and played some admirable football in the European Cup, the following season. An unfailingly cool, strong, yet scrupulously fair player who reads the game with great intelligence, tackles and intercepts splendidly, brings the ball out of defence well. His one full cap so far was won at Wembley in the unaccustomed position of right-back, against Northern Ireland, in 1972.

FRANJO VLADIC (Velez and Yugoslavia)
This blond inside-forward was a few days short of his twenty-second birthday when he made his debut for Yugoslavia against England at Wembley in October, 1972; with extraordinary success. He scored his team's goal, in the second half, with an accurate header, but would have had two or three more, were it not for the admirable saves of Peter Shilton, against his equally remarkable finishing. A complete inside-forward who can play in midfield but come through strongly for a crack at goal, he combines sweetly with his club mate, Bajevic.

HERBERT WIMMER (Borussia Moenchengladbach and West Germany) Another German player perfectly suited to 'total football'. Wimmer was originally an outside-right, and was devastatingly effective on the right wing against Belgium in the semi-final of the 1972 Nations Cup, in Antwerp. Yet he is just as impressive in midfield, using his ball control, pace and eye for an opening. In the Nations Cup Final, he briskly scored his team's second goal against Russia. Born on November 11, 1944, he came to Borussia Moenchengladbach from the Borussia Brand club, in 1966.

Georg Schwarzenbeck . . . 'ready and eager to break upfield'.

BY
ANTAL DUNAI
**UPJEST DOZSA and
HUNGARY**

'MAGICAL MAGYARS' — NOT SO EASY NOW

FOR some years past the Hungarian game has been in a state of flux and only now is a new style of play being developed that I think can bring success. In the 'fifties the Hungarian national team was outstanding and players like Ferenc Puskas, Jozsef Bozsik, and Nandor Hidegkuti were technically brilliant. I saw them as a teenager, though they all played before my time.

I may be wrong, but I am not sure that the team of the 'fifties would be quite so outstanding today. The game has changed. Perfect technique is not enough, as I think it might have been then.

When Hungarian football lost all its big personalities there followed a period in which the new players

Good action shot from a top Hungarian League game; it's Antal Dunai (left) beaten in the air by M.T.K. goalkeeper Hajdu. 'Personally, I am very optimistic for the future of the game in Hungary' says Dunai.

were not as good, and athletic qualities were stressed. In terms of speed and stamina our game improved, but the skill of the players was not as high.

Now I believe we have found the middle way; balancing the traditional Hungarian skill with modern training methods to produce the necessary physical qualities. Personally, I am very optimistic for the future of the game in Hungary. All we lack now, with a high level of play generally, is a few really outstanding individuals.

Not surprisingly, the interest shown by the public has declined. I think for a start there is too much football on television, but there are other factors. Living standards are higher, and people are much more comfortable. More people have cars and country cottages where they can spend their weekends. Football and other sports are not the only form of amusement or entertainment, as they once were.

It is also true that football as a whole is not as attractive as it was. Twenty years ago the emphasis was on skill and technique. Now the tendency is towards defence. This helps to keep the crowds down. The public wants to see skilful attacking movements and lots of goals, while tactically the game has become more defensive.

The future of the game is indicated I believe by two teams that have impressed me greatly, Ajax Amsterdam at club level, and, in the international arena, West Germany. For Ajax the outstanding players are Cruyff and Keizer, but the team is based on a very modern conception of the game. They have an outstanding style about their play, and well-balanced tactics similar to the West Germans. Beckenbauer, Netzer, and Müller are the key men in the West German team. In both sides the players have excellent physical condition, as well as skill; and the players don't worry too much about the numbers on their backs.

With Ajax and West Germany, defenders can go forward and shoot at goal while the forwards also have defensive responsibilities. This is team-work *par excellence*, the very best in modern football, giving the players more freedom of action, more room to express themselves, and not shackling them by giving the individuals fixed tasks which they must fulfil.

At international level, we Hungarians seem to have adopted a great inferiority complex. The newspapers appear to rate the professional players of other countries much too highly and are too critical of Hungarians. Whatever the reason, I have noticed over and over again that before big games the Hungarian players are pessimistic about their chances.

Once the game has started and they realise that their opponents are not as good as they thought there is a different mood, but by then it is often too late.

Another factor that works against Hungarian football is the timing of the most important matches. The quarter-finals of the big European competitions always come up in March at a time when the Hungarians, like everyone else in Eastern Europe, are only just starting to play again. The best teams of Holland, England, and Italy, on the other hand, are right at their peak at this time and still in top form.

Trying to counter this, we Hungarians have often toured South America and other exotic countries in the middle of what is our winter. No doubt it helps to prepare the players for the big games in March and April but I don't feel it is the best preparation. When I was younger, I used to look forward to travelling abroad, particularly to South America, where everything is so different. But these

Yes, a little girl is very proud of big brother – Dunai celebrates his sister's seventh birthday.

tours are too long and involve too much travelling. The result is often counter-productive, because the players come back physically and mentally tired.

I think it would be better to have good training at home in Hungary and play a few friendly matches that do not involve too much travelling. Things are improving. We are getting the balance right in the Hungarian game.

For myself, I am studying at the High School for Physical Education in Budapest. After a four-year course I hope to be a fully-qualified football trainer. Thirty years old, and with nearly 300 League games behind me, I hope to stay in the game and contribute something.

One of our big problems in Hungary is the lack of self-confidence, as I have already said. This comes in a large part from over-critical articles written by our sports press. The journalists are probably right, because they want to have a higher standard of play, but I think they are sometimes too critical.

What I dislike most are the jokes about Hungarian football. These days you can hardly go to a theatre or cabaret without hearing comedians telling jokes about how bad Hungarian football is. If the newspaper critics have a point in asking for a higher standard of play they should, I think, be a little more generous with their praise when Hungarian teams do well or when Hungarian players score good goals.

Certainly they give credit where it is due, but after a good Hungarian goal they give only a few nice words whereas they can write poetry about goals scored by top foreign stars.

The result is that I often find that foreign journalists give more praise to Hungarians than our own sportswriters do. What we really need is a better balanced standard of reporting with constructive criticism but also a fair measure of praise when it has been earned.

I've had my share of international goals and some of them have given me a great deal of satisfaction. Perhaps the most pleasing goal was one I scored in

1969 in the quarter-finals of the Inter Cities Fairs Cup. Away to Leeds United in the quarter-final first leg, I got a pass from Arpad Fazekas, feinted to go one way, and then shot from about 20 yards. It was the only goal of the game and we beat Leeds 3–0 on aggregate to go on and reach the Final.

Another fond memory of mine came in the qualifying matches for the 1970 World Cup. Unfortunately, although I was fortunate enough to have a good game, scoring two goals myself and laying on a pass for a third we didn't qualify. Beating the Czechs 3–1 at one stage, they came back to draw. After that we needed a play-off to settle the group and the Czechs beat us 4–1 in the decisive game in Marseille.

Still I've come a long way from Gara, a little village in Southern Hungary where I was born. The local Third Division team Bajai-Bacska was my first Club. From there I joined Pecsi Dozsa where for one season I played with my elder brother Janos (Dunai I). He played for Hungary in the Rome Olympics. Then I moved on to Ujpest Dozsa.

I've had a good run in top-class football and obtained a great deal of satisfaction and pleasure from playing. When I've finished as a player I hope to have finished my studies, become a coach and give something back to football.

Into Europe, again and again! (Right) It's Birmingham goal-getter Bob Latchford holding off Sampdoria of Genoa defender Negrisold. (Below) Willie Johnston soars to beat Moscow Dynamo's defence and score a second goal for Rangers.

END F.A. CONTROL OF NATIONAL XI
—'fair pay for fair play'

By JOHAN CRUYFF
Ajax-Amsterdam and Holland

IN my opinion people make a great mistake when they try to suggest that football is somehow 'inferior', possibly because it is the sport of the common people. Opera and the Theatre receive huge government subsidies, but ordinary people – myself included – don't go to the Opera. It is the people who occupy the higher positions in society who make up the audiences at Opera, Ballet and the Theatre. In any case, I don't think these top people like football.

Three hundred million people – ordinary people – sat watching the European Cup Final on television and whatever the society people think, my Ajax colleagues and I were the ambassadors of Holland that night.

When I read in the newspapers that another Dutch player has been transferred to a foreign team I ask myself what's wrong. I realised four years ago that something is wrong with the system in Holland. Every player that leaves the country proves my opinion.

Moment of elation for former Ajax Coach Rinus Michels: 'He gave us all a lot of understanding and technical knowledge' says Johan Cruyff.

You can't really blame good players for going abroad if they can because personal taxation is terribly high in Holland. Just imagine that Feyenoord could lose Wim van Hanegem to a foreign club. It would be a disaster for Feyenoord, and in my opinion the taxation system should be changed to encourage such players to stay in Holland.

As a professional football player my career will be over in about ten years and after that I become just an ordinary person again. Yet while I am at my peak and earning good money I have to pay an awful lot of taxes and it would be much fairer if the system were changed so that my taxes were related to average earnings over the whole of my working life instead of taking these ten good years separately.

Many people who study at the University earn very little before they are thirty years old but after that they do very well for the rest of their lives. With footballers, life is good at the beginning and then for all too many it means an automatic return to obscurity and ordinary work when their playing careers are over. Don't misunderstand me. I'm not asking for special treatment for Cruyff. I'm not too greedy to pay taxes. But I do think that the system could be made fairer to footballers by spreading the tax load over the whole working life, as for other workers.

Footballers are always being made aware that they are not just playing football as an activity in itself but providing entertainment and recreation for thousands of people. For the general public, football is a pleasant change from their everyday lives and also a hobby. That's what I think of as recreation and I feel we play an important role in society by providing this entertainment and relaxation.

I've heard it said that on Mondays, the workers are worth nothing because all they do is talk about the game they saw the day before. Critics claim the workers should be thinking about social problems but my answer is a simple one: if people think only about their work and social problems then they have no life at all. Everyone needs some joy in their life. Looking at things on this basis I feel the public has the right to demand everything I and other players can give on Sundays.

I remember once playing when I felt very ill indeed. I had a high temperature but I played even though the Club doctor said that I shouldn't. I don't think the public should be told this all the time; every week professionals play when they are ill or have not really recovered from injuries received in earlier matches, and so on. But I do think the public should be made aware that we earn a lot of

money largely because our earning years are so short.

Some have said professional players should study, or learn another profession, so that they can do something else after they quit football. But in my opinion that is unrealistic, in fact, almost impossible. If I have to prepare myself physically and mentally for every game, how can I sit with a book in my hands studying until an hour before the kick-off? If I am going to play well I have to concentrate and build myself up ready for the game.

I think this failure to understand the physical and mental strains on a professional is behind the widely-held belief that footballers are dumb; unfit for any responsible job when they return at 30 or so to normal life. The only logical solution is for the players to save as much money as they can during their playing career but high taxes make that very difficult.

I always ask for money when journalists want to interview me on subjects that have nothing to do with the actual playing of the game. The news-

Wim van Hanegem (left) heads for goal for Feyenoord against AC Milan. 'To lose Van Hanegem would be a disaster for Feyenoord' says Cruyff. (Top) Cruyff himself (centre, light shirt) for once comes off worst in this Dutch League match tussle.

papers don't publish stories about me because I am such a nice fellow but simply because I play football. I have a terribly nice neighbour who works very hard at his job but nobody writes articles about him!

Newspaper readers would not be interested in my neighbour, but I am well-known and therefore a good subject about which to write. Footballers are public figures and I feel people are entitled to know more about them. That is why I always agree to interviews. When journalists ask how are my children, I tell them, and even let them see them and photograph them.

My friend and Ajax colleague Piet Keizer is a bit more reticent and doesn't say too much to newspapermen. But I allow them into the privacy of my home and let them look around. Yet there are certain areas that I don't think should be public knowledge, for example how much money I give my wife for housekeeping.

I never react to things that are written about me, though perhaps I did a few years ago. I think that's a question of age and maturity. If I am playing badly I don't expect the newspapers to say that I played well. But instead of wide criticism I think it would be kinder if they wrote 'He had a bad day', a much kinder way of putting it.

Football is one of the most difficult professions. Just imagine having to live seven days preparing for the combat between two o'clock and four o'clock every Sunday. To me the biggest thing is the joy of playing but there are times when it really is hard work. When we go away for three days in a special training camp I often think 'Jesus! Away from home again. Three days without seeing the kids'.

I accept it is my profession, and it is my problem. If I order a plumber to come to my house I don't ask him how difficult his life is and I don't say, 'Hey, plumber, do this job the way I think it should be done'. What people generally fail to understand is that I am really just an ordinary worker. I don't sit around all day resting in an arm-chair.

Money doesn't really interest me as money. This may sound silly but it's true. The importance of money to me is simply that other people think it is important, so it must be important for me, too. I am asked for money all the time; when I buy a pair of shoes for the kids, or take a holiday, or want to buy a

British football's newest 'Superstar' – Kevin Keegan of Liverpool, who effortlessly took over the mantle thrown aside by George Best. (Top right) Keegan in England shirt comes in crabwise to Wales 'keeper Gary Sprake, but fails to get the ball past him. (Below) Another 'near miss' – Keegan just fails to get a touch to this ball as it runs wide, with Manchester City 'keeper Joe Corrigan beaten.

new car. I don't need a Rolls Royce. Just a nice car will do me, and I'd like to give my children a good education.

Such talk about money might seem a bit unpleasant, but I am not really like that. When I am sitting with a drink in my hands in a comfortable chair in the garden I am perfectly content. What more could I want? You can't drink two bottles at once.

As a player I think you can always improve, though in my opinion players reach their peak around 27. I realise that my heading ability could be better and I do work for improvement. Of course I can head a ball all right but I'm not particularly good at it, and quite often I have very bad headaches all day after playing a game and heading a heavy ball.

As I have often said I really love football. Enjoying it and getting joy out of it is what the game is all about to me. Most of the time training is enjoyable, too, but when I have to run for half-an-hour around the pitch then I recognise that it is a hard profession. At the beginning of the season, when we go to a training camp I find it is a lousy profession, too. On the field of play it is a joy, but particularly at the start of the season, preparation for it is really hard work.

The former Ajax Coach Rinus Michels gave us all a lot of understanding and technical knowledge. At first we all had an awful lot to learn about the game, and he helped tremendously. Now we are taking advantage of everything he gave us. Basically we all as individual players have our own prescribed assignment for each match, but at Ajax we play without rigid instructions.

The playing of the individual remains important and it must always I think be possible to be creative. The big thing about Ajax now is that everyone knows what to do – with or without the ball – whatever the situation. The forwards know that they cannot allow enemy defenders to attack without trying to stop them and in the same way our defenders know that they are accepting risks when they go upfield to try and score or help to score a goal. We play as individuals but within a team framework.

It seems to me that if players are bogged down with pre-match tactical instructions then the game becomes less attractive to watch. Most of the time I do things that I feel should be done.

The other players are the same, I feel sure. The individual has to make decisions but above all the results depend on team-work. Most clubs, specially in Holland don't have professional football in this

Fanfare for Europe! – though that's nothing new for football. Nevertheless, Britain, Denmark, and Eire – 'The Three' newcomers to the Common Market – scored a 2–0 win over 'The Six' present members at Wembley. Danish winger Henning Jensen scores the first goal against Italian goalkeeper Dino Zoff.

sense. In many clubs there is a kind of very nervous 'knocking on the door' of professional football. This is because the officials and administrators are amateurs or, if they are paid, they think like amateurs.

So many officials think they are very important and their attitude to the players is: 'We have ten minutes to spare. Let the boy say something'!

Kevin Keegan climbing with Liverpool team-mate Chris Lawler trying to unsettle Crystal Palace 'keeper Jackson, being willed on by Mel Blyth (left).

Many people also feel they are not paid well enough compared to the players. Club secretaries, for example, often feel it is wrong that boys of 22 should earn more as players than they do at 40 or 50. Fortunately, we don't have such difficulties in our Club but we do have this kind of thing with the Dutch national team. I'm sure it would be much better in every way if the control of the national team was taken away from the Football Association.

My reason for thinking this way is the attitude of the FA officials. They seem to think players should be honoured to be given the chance to play in the Dutch team. I think this is a wrong attitude. It would be just as wrong if I said to them, 'You should be very happy having me play in the national team'.

At Ajax they do not tell me, 'Cruyff, you are lucky. You are allowed to play in this beautiful Stadium of ours.' Ajax run their club like a business undertaking that needs me as much as I need it.

Most players are far too dependent on their clubs. But I am an idealist who likes to play football, except in the month of June. That's the time when I have to negotiate my new contract with the Club, and then I am ready to fight for it.

It's the same kind of situation with the national team. I am playing in the team. So they advertise me; print my name in the programme; and the public give money to the FA to watch me and my team-mates. I feel that's OK; but I also think that I should be allowed to profit from it a little bit, too.

(Reproduced by permission of *De Volkskrant*, Amsterdam.)

Hey! that's no way to further an England career. Young England man Trevor Francis of Birmingham (left) hands off mighty England skipper Bobby Moore of West Ham, and steals away with the ball . . .

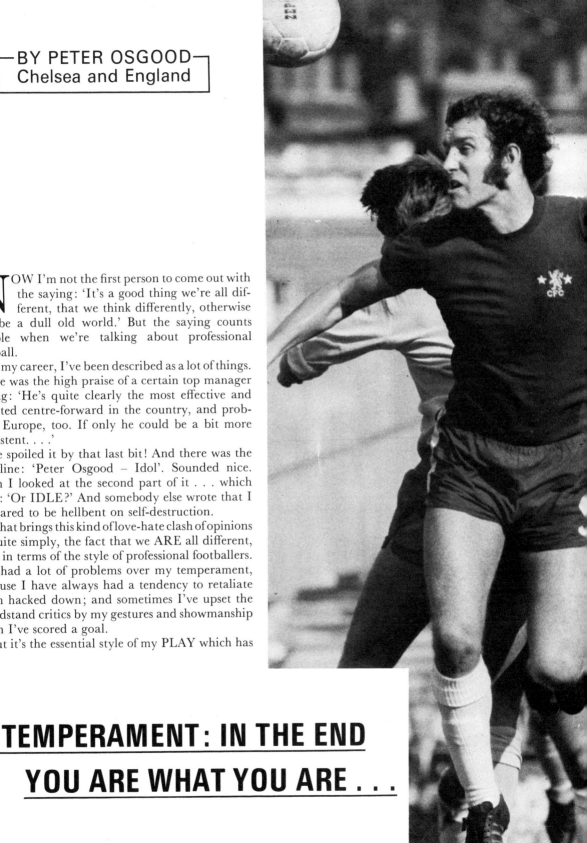

BY PETER OSGOOD
Chelsea and England

NOW I'm not the first person to come out with the saying: 'It's a good thing we're all different, that we think differently, otherwise it'd be a dull old world.' But the saying counts double when we're talking about professional football.

In my career, I've been described as a lot of things. There was the high praise of a certain top manager saying: 'He's quite clearly the most effective and talented centre-forward in the country, and probably Europe, too. If only he could be a bit more consistent. . . .'

He spoiled it by that last bit! And there was the headline: 'Peter Osgood – Idol'. Sounded nice. Then I looked at the second part of it . . . which read: 'Or IDLE?' And somebody else wrote that I appeared to be hellbent on self-destruction.

What brings this kind of love-hate clash of opinions is, quite simply, the fact that we ARE all different, even in terms of the style of professional footballers. I've had a lot of problems over my temperament, because I have always had a tendency to retaliate when hacked down; and sometimes I've upset the grandstand critics by my gestures and showmanship when I've scored a goal.

But it's the essential style of my PLAY which has

TEMPERAMENT: IN THE END
YOU ARE WHAT YOU ARE . . .

Human grapeshot, that's Steve Kember of Chelsea (left) as he lets fly this header past an equally agile Leicester defender. (Facing page) Mel Blyth of Crystal Palace brings a dropping-jaw look of surprise from Chelsea's Bill Garner as he heads this one away brilliantly.

brought the greatest amount of criticism. There are players who get out on the park and never stop running. One thinks of a Kevin Keegan or a Frannie Lee. There are others whose style is not that way at all – players who appear a bit languid, or lazy . . . or idle, if you will. It's definitely not my style to tear around for ninety minutes. That may have kept me out of a regular place in the England squad, but I am what I am.

When I first got into the Chelsea side, back in the 1965–66 season, I realised that you do have to take the rough with the smooth in this game. At Stamford Bridge, it was great to hear the Shed supporters shouting 'Osgood IS good' on behalf of a youngster not long off the building sites near home at Windsor. Then the team would go up North where the crowds took great delight in yelling 'Osgood NO good'.

But you soon learn to take that kind of comment. I relished those moments when I could retaliate with the odd forceful gesture in the direction of the

opposition terraces when the ball slid handsomely into the net. That got me a little more criticism, because it was said that I lacked balance – couldn't take the transition from amateur football with Spital Old Boys to the cream of the First Division.

I got seven goals in my first season. Only six in the next, but then I'd broken my leg after a tackle involving Emlyn Hughes (who was then with Blackpool) . . . a fifty-fifty ball, and my right leg went home, and I had some terribly dark thoughts about whether I'd be another Alick Jeffrey, out of the game almost before his career had started.

However, I'm only too aware what my faults are. I know that I've got a lot of skill in the air, and I've got excellent balance and control on the deck, but there is this tendency to drift in and out of the game more than I should. More, indeed, that I really like to.

Perhaps, right from the start, it was a lack of concentration. A big build-up continued to the

Football, or a spot of all-in wrestling? — whatever, it seems to be amusing Chelsea's Chris Garland (dark shirt) as he scissors Ipswich centre-half Jefferson.

Surely one of the best football pictures of the year — it's the comeback game (and two goals to mark it!) of Chelsea's Ian Hutchinson, here seen sliding away from under the oncoming boot of a Norwich defender.

utumn of 1971 when manager Dave Sexton put
e on the transfer list. He said he wasn't satisfied
ith my performances, and that must have sounded
o all the world as if I hadn't been trying.

Certainly it bucked me up and for a while after
oming off the list I have no doubt I really *was*
oing a lot of running off the ball. But in the end,
ou are what you are. I've my strengths, and I
now all about my weaknesses.

I've got my height – around 6 ft 2 in. – and I can
me a jump well. And on the ground, I've always
ad the ability to find the time for a shot or a cross.
ut if my passing is accurate, and so is my shooting,
he honest truth is that I don't have that kind of
hunderbolt shot that men like Bobby Charlton

could produce from thirty yards out.

Most of the time, I need to get as near goal as
possible. Through the years, it's been very rare for
me to score from outside the area. But any professional owes it to himself to work on the weak points,
and many's the hour I've spent shooting in from
outside the box. Same with my right foot being by
far the stronger; I still keep trying to get my left
leg up to standard.

There's no point me getting into an argument
with my critics. If they think I look slow and lazy
from the Press box, then fair enough. But I'll never
be a sprinter. I have long legs, which makes it *look*
as if I'm going slower than other players. But, again,
I think there are different ways of getting into posi-

Chelsea's David Webb (left) and Chris Garland get in among the Leicester defence, but whatever'
going on the referee has his hand up, and is about to put a stop to it! (Right) Webb a spectator thi
time, as the Chelsea right back makes things hot for Everton's outside-right.

tion – you can make it by non-stop running, or you can 'think' ahead far enough to get there.

And I've talked to goalkeepers and I know that I make it difficult for them to know which way I'm going to shoot. Once I've got the ball in a good position, I can shield it, then slide it. At that range, you've got virtually the whole goal to go for.

I look at my career so far and I listen to the people who say I've not made the best of my opportunities and I just wonder. After all, I have played for England at full and Under-23 level, and there were the Football League games, and there have been the travels with Chelsea . . . winning the FA Cup after that replay against Leeds United; going on to the European Cup-Winners' Cup. Maybe I could have been an England 'regular', but I wouldn't blame Sir Alf Ramsey for not making me one.

As I was saying earlier, it takes all sorts of player to make up a game of football. And if my 'sor wasn't the kind Sir Alf was looking for . . . wel that didn't mean that I was useless at the game, o boring to watch.

Those gestures of mine? Well, they started a genuine expressions of anger. In the days before th tackle from behind was cut out, it was difficult fo players like me to play the ball through withou being smashed across the legs. Week after week, ball would be played up to me, and I'd go to knoc it back to a colleague . . . and then get heavily take from behind for my pains.

So . . . along come the bookings. And in the en comes the suspension. I've had more than my shar of trouble, but I'd definitely deny any theory tha I've ever been a dirty player. Did you know, fo example, that Arsenal striker John Radford use wear shinpads on the *back* of his legs?

I suppose some of us are guilty of living up to an image. I make those little gestures, clown around a bit, get over-excited . . . but what looks bad from the terraces may be just a little joke out there on the park.

Sometimes, though I wonder if things would have been different if I *had* been born with that intense kind of concentration, that 100 per cent physical effort of non-stop running, that some players produce.

At Chelsea, there is John Hollins, for instance. He's the original 90-minute non-stop clockwork wind-up man, who inspires the team by his efforts and by his vocal backchat when things are going wrong. A good leader is John. A good skipper. I don't think there's much danger of *my* kind of player being picked for qualities of leadership.

I think, too, of Ian Hutchinson, who has to be one of the bravest strikers ever in the game. All those terrible injuries which have threatened his career -- but when he's there, and fit, he turns on magnificently physical, always challenging, performances. A lot of my goals have been push-ins, after big Hutch has made the big through run, torn the first big gap in the opposition.

That's why it's such a good thing that it takes all sorts to make a world, especially in top-class Soccer. A team made up of robot-like similar types wouldn't do a lot for the spectators. But a team of different characters, different personalities, can be very interesting to watch.

The non-stop runners feed off us 'lazy' types. And we in turn are inspired by the sprinters.

Without those different types, it really would be a dull old footballing world!

SCOTLAND'S BIG HOPE IS BRITISH LEAGUE

—says MARTIN BUCHAN of Manchester United and Scotland

UNDOUBTEDLY there's a bigger market for football in England than there is in Scotland but Soccer south of the border is bigger in every way. More thought goes into the game, and team planning is more thorough throughout the First Division. In Scotland only about six clubs really work at the game in the same way as the English.

Lack of support and the cash shortage this brings is the root problem. People who live in Glasgow and its environs for example, travel to see Rangers and Celtic play away rather than go to watch other clubs in the area. In this way teams like Motherwell, Partick Thistle, Kilmarnock, and Clyde lose out to the pull of the two giants.

In the case of Aberdeen, where I played before being transferred to Manchester United, the nearest First Division football is played in Dundee which is more than sixty miles away. So Aberdeen has a big area from which to draw support, but in recent years this potential has not been reflected in the size of attendances at Pittodrie Stadium.

Times have changed since the days when the match on Saturday was the highlight of the working man's week. People have more scope for pursuing other interests and thousands today play golf or go fishing at weekends and many more must spend Saturday afternoons watching the sports programmes on television.

Martin Buchan in action for Manchester United soon after his transfer from Aberdeen.

As far as the immediate future in Scotland is concerned, I think Hibernians can offer a serious challenge to Celtic. Hibs are one of the few really well-organised clubs. Their manager, Eddie Turnbull, was my boss at Aberdeen and he travelled widely in England and West Germany studying the game and training methods. Hibernians are getting the benefit of all he has seen and learned. Generally, Scottish clubs have perhaps three or four above-average players, whereas in England the overall standard is much higher. The top English clubs may have as many as six or seven players in this category and there are very good players even in the bottom teams in the English First Division. Scottish clubs continue to find above-average players but their problems revolve around the difficulties of keeping them. Not long ago, the best Scottish players drifted naturally towards Rangers and Celtic. Now the tendancy is towards English First Division clubs and the drift has become intensified.

Pat Stanton, of Hibernians, has always been a quality player though he has obviously benefited from the influence of Eddie Turnbull. For Aberdeen the outstanding player now is the Hungarian inside-forward Zoltan Varga. In my time with Aberdeen Joe Harper was outstanding for his goalscoring ability, but an extremely underrated player, in my opinion, was full-back Jim Hermiston. Dave Robb was also a very valuable team player.

The tragedy for Aberdeen and the majority of the other Scottish sides is that they are eventually forced to part with such players for reasons of pure economics. The total population of Scotland is something over five million and that just isn't enough to support a full First Division. By comparison with English football, the Scottish game lacks atmosphere. There are fewer important League matches to keep players on their toes every week. I must say, however, in fairness, that facilities at Pittodrie, Ibrox, and Parkhead compare favourably with anything I have seen in England.

I was born in Aberdeen and was still at school when I made up my mind to become a professional. I had been connected with the club since I was 12 years old and at 17 I was undecided between professional football and a University education. Needing one more subject for the University Entrance standard, I intended to stay on at school for a sixth year but I was lucky enough to get a

Keeping top-class men north of the border is Scotland's big problem, says Martin Buchan: but the standards of the 'Old Firm' remain high and very, very competitive — as witness the determination in the faces of Celtic's George Connelly (left) and Rangers' Willie Johnston.

game in Aberdeen's reserves before the school term started. After a few days back at school I decided to join Aberdeen as a full-time professional but took steps to continue my education by enrolling in an Evening Class course. When the time came around for the examinations, however, I was away in the United States with Aberdeen.

I played four times in Aberdeen's first team in that first season after school but it took two years and a recovery from a broken ankle before I became a regular first-team player.

My international experience is somewhat limited. My first cap came in a European Championship game against Belgium at Aberdeen's Pittodrie Stadium, where we won 1–0 through a goal from John O'Hare. I've been in the Scottish squad since then and I'd dearly like to play in the World Cup. Everyone in Scotland is optimistic about our chances of qualifying.

Having beaten Denmark twice I feel we are half way there and the general opinion seems to be that the Danes can help out by taking a point or even two from Czechoslovakia when they meet in Copenhagen. If that should happen, Scotland could then qualify by beating the Czechs at Hampden Park.

From the fans' viewpoint, the annual match with England is the big thing but that will surely take second place in 1973 as Scotland strives to qualify for the World Cup finals for the first time since 1958.

In my opinion, the English domestic game offers a higher standard of competition because of the presence in England of many players from Scotland, Northern Ireland, the Republic, and Wales. Scottish clubs lose out here again because they find it difficult to persuade top-class players to go and play north of the border.

Zoltan Varga, who joined Aberdeen in September 1972, is, of course, an outstanding exception. There were various opinions about the rights and wrongs of the part he was alleged to have played in the bribery scandal in West Germany. But everyone who has seen him play – as I did on New Year's Day – must agree that he is a world-class player. His greatest attribute is his skill and, following from that, the confidence he has in his ability to make the ball do exactly as he wants.

Among the Scottish clubs, only the top six would have any chance of doing well in the English First Division. Economics are the 'crunch' for the game in Scotland; and already several clubs are being forced to cut down the numbers of full-time professionals.

The future looks bleak. Will the crowds come back? I do not think so. If new stadia with modern, comfortable, conditions for the spectator had been built a few years ago then it might have been different. That, allied to a reconstructed, more competitive League system might have kept the interest of the public alive. Now the big hope for the top Scottish teams must be the formation of a British League.

As for myself, I'm happy to be a player and hope to go on playing and enjoying the game for a good few years yet. When the time comes to quit I'd like to stay in the game in some capacity. I wonder what will the game be like when that time comes

A 'golden touch'? – a touch, certainly, by Crystal Palace £115,000 signing Ian Phillips, playing it 'back to back' with Norwich's Jim Bone.

GOALS?—I JUST DON'T HAVE THAT MAGICAL 'KNACK'

Head's management and we played some good football, too. I was lucky enough to get my chance early: I was in the reserve team at 15 and the first XI when only 16. Among those I played with at Swindon were Don Rogers, now at Crystal Palace, and Ernie Hunt, who played later for Wolves, Everton, and Coventry City.

There was always talk about transfers in those

> **BY MIKE SUMMERBEE**
> **Manchester City and England**

days, but nothing happened until we were relegated to the Third Division. Then I asked for a move and came to join Manchester City. Don Rogers stayed on and I left, but in the end I think things worked out well for us both.

Before I finish playing I'd very much like to win the First Division Championship again. I'm not greedy and I've already won nearly every honour going, but my only real ambition is to stay on with Manchester City and help them win the League. When I'm not good enough to play for City, then I'll quit.

I'VE been around a long time, I suppose, because I was lucky to get off to a good start with Swindon. I played as a youngster for a team called Baker Street YMCA in the Cheltenham League and a man called Cecil Green, who is now a director of Swindon, took me to the Club.

We had a lot of good young players under Bert

I don't feel there is any point in going into a lower Division looking for something that isn't there. When the writing is on the wall I'm sure I'll see it and get out–but my last game will be for City.

We could and perhaps should have won the League again in the 1971–72 season, when we made up quite a gap between us and Manchester United but got pipped at the end. The title went to Derby. I really think it was our own fault. We should have won. It was there for the taking; we had only to win our last two games to be Champions. The first of these was at home to Stoke City and we murdered them for football but lost 2–1, and that was it.

Basically, I can play anywhere up front, though I'm a right-sided player by nature and I prefer outside-right. I was a right-winger when I first played for City, but was moved to centre forward. I enjoyed it, but I prefer playing on the wing. My three England caps came at centre forward, but only managed to score one goal; a header in the 1– draw against Switzerland at Wembley.

This inability to score goals is my biggest fault.

It's one thing to know your faults but quite another to do something about them. I've never been known as a goal-scorer, which may seem strange for some one who has played regularly at centre-forward. I'm no Pelé, not even a Jairzinho, who also switched from centre-forward to the right-wing but still get goals.

I don't move inside enough looking for goals. But I'm a strong runner and I don't think there's many First Division backs who stop me regularly. If I don't get goals myself I think I can say that other people get goals off me. That's what really counts.

It can be a bit painful, this growing-up business; sometimes you can grow right out of your favourite job. That's what happened to Manchester City mascot Paul Todd, aged 12, below. After seven years in the job – which took him to virtually every First Division ground – he has been gently retired. He says goodbye to Mike Summerbee, Rodney Marsh, Mike Doyle, and Francis Lee. (Facing page) It's a case of 'Where'd he go?!' as Coventry's Brian Alderson hurdles Manchester City 'keeper Ron Healey, Olympic-style.

It doesn't matter who gets the goals as long as they go in.

One of the goals I did get stands out in my memory. It was the day we clinched the League Championship. We were playing Newcastle and after three minutes Colin Bell came down the right and hit the ball hard and low. It bobbled a couple of times, came through a crowd of players, and I flicked it in. I knew it was a goal the moment I touched it and it gave us just the start we needed.

We went on to win by four goals to three . . . and take the Championship. It wasn't a fantastic goal or anything like that, but it was a vital one, and it counted. Of course, scoring goals isn't everything, even at centre forward. You need a special kind of gift and a special temperament to be a regular scorer and I just don't seem to have it. Like taking penalty kicks. I've never been asked to take one but I'm sure you need a certain gift to be good at it and score regularly.

Playing up front you are always dependent on the service you get from the other players around you.

You can't have a good game if you don't see much of the ball. This is specially true at centre-forward where if you get plenty of the ball you can have a real influence on the outcome of the game and the way it is played. You can't possibly have the same degree of influence playing on the wing but you can still do things as long as people play to you.

You're not involved all the time as you are at centre-forward but it can still be satisfying on the wing. As long as you see plenty of the ball you can have a say in which way the game goes. But you are still dictated to by the people around you and you rely on them playing well, just as they rely on me. But on the wing everything depends on the service you get.

Things have worked out well for me since I left Swindon and I've enjoyed every minute of it. As I said before I'm not greedy but I would like to help City win the League once more before I end my career. And I've quite made up my mind. My last game will be for Manchester City.

I FOUND MY 'KILLER INSTINCT' AT NO. 9

BY MALCOLM MACDONALD
Newcastle United and England

I AM what I would call a hundred per cent man, the one with the responsibility for putting the ball in the net and finishing off the work of all the other players. It's a big responsibility, but I thrive on it. It doesn't worry me one bit.

When I was transferred from Luton Town to Newcastle United for a big fee many critics wondered whether I could make the grade as a striker in the top class. It seemed to me at the time – not knowing how our manager Mr. Harvey felt – that I was the only one who wasn't worried.

I've always had a philosophical approach to the game, plus a great determination to succeed. When I joined Newcastle United, surely one of the most affluent clubs in the Football League, I felt I was ready. No one else really knew how deep and long my apprenticeship was.

How could they? I was an unknown when I learned the most important things in the game, and my progress was timed just right. Before I moved to Newcastle I'd had a real grounding in the fundamentals of the game, playing in almost every position and meeting all kinds of experiences. I felt I was ready.

While others were wondering if I could score goals in the faster, more competitive, First Division,

Down, but not out – though floored, Steve Perryman of Spurs halts Manchester City's Francis Lee.

Malcolm Macdonald (left) . . . a nodding acquaintance with Chelsea's David Webb.

instance, during my spell with Tonbridge the Club went through a hard time and all the players were asked to take a cut in wages. At the time I was getting a basic £10 a week plus £2 for a win and £1 for a draw. Playing three times a week that could make your money something worthwhile. When financial difficulties overtook the club I was getting only my basic wage which, after tax, meant that I got about £7.50 a week.

I was quietly confident. I remember thinking to myself of the time when I faced a real challenge way back in my early days with Tonbridge.

I was a Southern League player then, and seventeen years old. I learned a lot around that time, perhaps because I had to. I went virtually straight from schoolboy football into the Southern League with only my enthusiasm for the game and the confidence of my manager, Harry Haslam, to help me.

Harry has been a tremendous help to me in my career, taking me with him when he moved from Tonbridge to Fulham and then to Luton. I owe him a great deal; as I do my mother, who made it possible for me to play three times a week for Tonbridge in my early days.

I was born at Fulham but my father died when I was 16 and my mother moved to a small place in Sussex, where she bought a shop. I used to work in the shop but as often happened, when I needed time off to travel to away games, particularly in midweek, it was my mother who took on the whole load of the shop. If I'd been in a regular job working steady hours I'd have found it very difficult to get all the time off I needed to play for Tonbridge. Probably, I would never had finished up in the First Division.

Looking back, I've had my ups and downs. For

Tommy Gibbs, in action for Newcastle . . . 'If he hadn't played football for a living I'm sure he'd have won an Olympic Gold Medal for something. That's the kind of man Tommy is'.

With Tonbridge, I think the most important thing I learned was how to look after myself. You had to learn quickly at 17, playing in that kind of football every week against teams that had a good sprinkling of former Football League-club players.

When Harry Haslam moved to Fulham, he persuaded the manager, Bobby Robson, to sign me on. At that time I had been played by Harry in almost every position but I had played mostly at right-back. I joined Fulham at the start of the pre-season training and played in quite a few friendlies at full-back.

Then when the competitive games began the Club was plagued by a glut of injuries to forwards, and Harry said to Bobby Robson, 'Play Malcolm as a forward'. I remember I scored five goals in five games for the reserves and then, with Fulham still suffering from injuries, I got a chance in the first team and scored five more goals in eight League games.

It was almost the same at Luton. First Harry Haslam went; and then he suggested to the manager, Alec Stock, that he have a look at me. So I followed Harry again, and at Luton I began once more as a full-back. This time, after only two friendly matches, our left-winger was injured during the game. Harry suggested to Alec Stock that he should try me there. He did, and presumably liked the way I played. After that I stayed as the nominal winger – with an 11 on my back, and

Bobby Moncur, Newcastle's fine Scot (right) . . . 'I have the greatest respect for all my colleagues' says Macdonald. (Below) Fulham manager Alec Stock . . . 'He switched me to centre-forward'.

playing a roving game in attack. Finally, again because of injuries, I was switched to centre-forward. There I stayed until I was transferred to Newcastle.

At the time of my move it was said that I was a converted full-back, but that really wasn't quite true. It would be more accurate to say that I was a player who had played in every position, including goal, and played most often at full-back. But I was a player rather than a back until Luton decided to keep me at centre-forward.

Now I am accepted as a centre-forward – a modern striker. Scoring goals to round off the work of the entire team is my role. I revel in it, but I realise all forwards are dependent on the players around them for their success. If you don't have wingers laying on crosses, and midfield players making runs and creating spaces for you to exploit, then the chances don't come. Strikers are only as good as the players around them, and I have the greatest respect for all my colleagues.

Perhaps I have the greatest respect of all for the coal miners who watch me do my job on Saturdays. They really work, going down the pit and grafting eight hours a day. This willingness to graft pervades everything in and around Newcastle, and perhaps inevitably it infects the local football club. I think the willingness to graft is personified by our Tommy Gibbs – a real 100 per cent man. If he hadn't played football for a living I'm sure he'd have won an Olympics Gold medal for something. That's the kind of man Tommy is.

I like to feel that I'm a 100 per cent man myself, too. I know my limitations, but I have speed and strength on my side and I love the responsibility for getting goals. When the chances come I think anyone that hesitates is lost and this is where I feel my 'killer' instinct is so valuable. In front of goal you have to be prepared to 'do or die', there's no second chance for those who think about getting hurt. You just dive in to get the ball in the net.

With Newcastle I think we've yet to show our real potential, but with England all I can say is that I'm always the super optimist.

Colin Bell scores for England against Wales – bringing a smile to Malcolm Macdonald (in background), and a frown to big Mike England, the Welsh centre-half.

'good football all the way . . .'

EIGHTEEN months ago I was playing in midfield for West Ham and though I enjoyed it and even managed to score a few goals going forward, I enjoyed last season best of all. For me, the most important and enjoyable thing is to score goals and playing up, as I am now, I get every opportunity to score.

Perhaps the most important thing I've learned about the game is the importance of following up shots – whether they are your own or hit by someone else. From the opposing goalkeeper's viewpoint this makes the vital difference.

A good shot can extend a goalkeeper without perhaps beating him, and then, if there's no one around, he'll feel confident and happy. He may not be able to hold the ball cleanly, maybe blocking the ball with his body or knocking the ball away; but, unchallenged, he can get a second chance to grab

BY BRYAN 'POP' ROBSON
of West Ham

the ball cleanly, and hold it.

With a player following up while the shot is actually on its way towards goal, the 'keeper has

IF WE MAKE IT, WEST HAM
WILL BE GREAT CHAMPIONS

to be much more on his toes. He knows that if he fails to hold the ball, there'll be no second chance. Putting pressure on goalkeepers in this way can unsettle them and force one or two errors that can mean goals.

I enjoyed my stint in midfield, although it was new to me. It took time to develop an understanding with my colleagues. But I never really got used to the need to discipline myself, because as a midfield player I inevitably got involved in marking opponents when we lost possession.

Playing up, as I am now, I do drop back to work because I enjoy my football and don't like to be out of the game for any length of time, but the midfield grafting I do now is done because I want to, or feel I ought to, and not because I have to.

The great joy in playing, and certainly the part I like best, is going forward. This is really what the game is all about and not being tied in any way at all I am free to look for opportunities inside the penalty box.

You cannot always predict how things will go for you. I had a part in success when I was with Newcastle, when we won the Fairs Cup. We beat the Hungarians Ujpest Dozsa in the Final, and put out Feyenoord on the way. The following season everyone expected us to do really well in the League. But it never quite worked out, perhaps because we were a bit too defensive.

Everyone was carried away with that Fairs Cup success and we had a tremendous team spirit. Success breeds team spirit, and the will to win, quicker than anything else I know. I think on balance we had a side ideally suited to two-legged Cup competitions with a tough, well-organised, defence that gave nothing away; but we lacked class in midfield. Our defence carried us through in the vital away games.

Newcastle are an altogether different outfit now. Malcolm Macdonald is the ideal type of centre-forward, and with Terry Hibbitt and Tony Green in midfield there's a much better balance. And they have Stuart Barraclough on the right wing – they never had a winger when I was there.

Since I joined West Ham, all the things I'd seen and heard about them, and thought to myself, about their style of play have been confirmed for me. Last season we put together some of the best football I've ever been involved with but somehow

Billy Bonds (on ground, left) manages to share a chuckle with Stoke's John Mahoney, even though he's having the worst of things. (Right) it seems as if Trevor Francis of Birmingham (in white, centre) is taking time out for a spot of ballet training, while West Ham's Clive Charles and Frank Lampard decide to get on with the game.

we just didn't get the results we deserved.

Our first three games produced some truly remarkable football with our games away to Liverpool and Arsenal absolutely sensational. To take Liverpool on at Anfield and deserve to win is no mean achievement and we really could – and should – have won there. Instead we lost 3–2 after being 2–1 up.

I think consistency is our big problem at West Ham, but we are getting better all the time as the younger players mature and grow in confidence. When I was first transferred to the 'Hammers' we used to produce some really good football for spells of 20 to 30 minutes and then fade. Now I feel we can do it for 50 to 60 minutes, and when you are closely involved with it, as I am, you can feel the mood. I'm sure we are very close to doing something really exceptional.

I remember when I first met Ron Greenwood. He came up to Newcastle to try and obtain my transfer and he told me that good football is a question of good habits. I had those habits, or many of them, naturally, he told me and said that I would fit in very quickly. I can testify how right he was. Though

I played in midfield at first, and I had not only to change my natural style but also develop an understanding with Billy Bonds and Trevor Brooking, I had no trouble settling in. Right away I was enjoying it.

Football-wise I've never regretted leaving Newcastle for West Ham. But I would dearly love to win the Championship. I'm sure Ron Greenwood wants it, too, but he's also after good football. He believes you have to keep the game simple, and try to play good football – and the team is doing just that. We are very close, but something still seems to be missing, though it might just be, as I said earlier, that it is concentration that is lacking.

What Mr. Greenwood is after is a team that can produce really good football and maintain it over 42 games. What he wants is to win the League playing good football, and you can't do anything but respect a man with principles like that.

Our training at West Ham is quite different from that I knew at Newcastle. To begin with, it's lighter – or seems to be – and we certainly do more work with the ball in three's. We do a lot of sprinting in small areas, making angles, jockeying, tackling, getting tight on people. You can do a lot of running that way, but it doesn't seem so much like hard work because it's done with the ball.

The training is basically split into two categories: three against three in tight areas, and six against six on a full pitch. Three against three is tight and quick, involving all the little intricacies of the game. Six against six is quite different. There you have time to think, look around and run with the ball. Running 50 yards with the ball, shooting and then having to run back another 50 yards can be pretty tiring, physically. But mentally it's quite different – and much more enjoyable.

For a player it's tremendous being a part of the set-up at West Ham. So many people say that Ron Greenwood is the best coach in the business – and I am sure he is. All the top teams in England are trying to copy him and that's the biggest compliment of all. Yet I'm sure he'd also love to get his hands on the League Championship Trophy . . . just as I would.

A goal against West Ham, and it proved the winner – so no wonder Liverpool's Kevin Keegan leaps for joy, with Chris Lawler helpfully waiting to catch him.

BY ED STEWART

top B.B.C. disc jockey

TO be in show-business, you've obviously got to be a bit of a show-off. It's not the shrinking violets who get their names in lights . . . though I suppose Greta Garbo didn't do so badly, come to think of it.

As a disc-jockey, I broadcast to audiences of up to *fifteen* million people. If I stopped to try and count all those people, I'd not only wear myself out, but I'd be scared stiff. When I'm working, I try to think that I'm just having a kindly chat with just *one* person.

I TALK TO MILLIONS, BUT HOW GOODISON SCARED ME !

But on personal appearances, I've faced thousands of faces, eyes glued on yours truly. And it still doesn't scare me. . . .

Yet when I trotted out for a game of football recently, and heard some of the kids watching chant my name, 'Stewpot, Stewpot,' I'll admit the old butterflies churned around in my tummy. Ed Stewart, professional show-off, used to crowds of all shapes and sizes, was dead scared.

Reason is, that I trotted out into the floodlit open space called Goodison Park. I'd organised the show-business side for a testimonial game for that great old Everton centre-half Brian Labone. And though I've been mustard-hot keen on all kinds of sport during my life, I'm potty about football – and a genuine raving nut about Everton.

Considering I was actually born in Wimbledon, which is down south, straight on past London, my obsession with Everton comes as a surprise to most people I meet. I went to school in Oxford, which isn't all that much nearer Liverpool. But my devo-tion to Everton came one Saturday afternoon when I was a six-year-old lad, off to see my first-ever football match . . . and saw Chelsea wallop the Everton side by six goals to nowt. One for each year of my life.

My brother John, who'd taken me to the ground, was a confirmed Chelsea man. Maybe it was the superior way he greeted each Chelsea goal, but it all conspired to make me the loudest-shouting Everton fan on the ground.

And that enthusiasm has simply got stronger over the years. I went to St Edward's, Oxford, and played rugger, hockey, cricket, and tennis . . . but I spent hours talking about football, Everton in particular. My best mate was a Manchester United addict, so we had some glorious arguments.

Even when Everton were in the Second Division, I shouted their praises. Those players of that era, goalkeeper Ted Sagar, big Tommy Jones in the middle of the defence, Peter Farrell, and Albert Dunlop. Dixie Dean, too – though I never saw him play. But I knew of his goal-scoring efforts for the 'world's finest soccer club', so I had no doubts that he was a true god in human form.

And when my educational days were over, I travelled round still spreading the gospel according to Everton football. I went to Singapore, then Hong Kong. I made a break into local radio there, but was 'forced' to commentate only on Rugby Union football. I spent a fortune on getting the English papers over as quickly as possible so I could read accounts of the Everton matches.

Back in England, I joined the so-called 'pirate' ship *Radio London*, spending weeks on end anchored at sea, but the brightest part of each week was hearing how Everton got on. I used to urge the players on, over the air . . . 'Everton for two points this afternoon, don't worry about that! And now a Cliff Richard record for Charlie So-and-so . . .'

Truth is, that through my support for Everton I was working off a bit of my frustration at never having really made the grade as a sportsman myself. I know there are millions who envy me the life of a disc-jockey, with the glamour and the fame and so on, but my own kicks come from meeting up with the Everton players (most of them are real mates of mine now). Just walking into a soccer dressing-room and getting a sniff at the embrocation . . . it's a world I would love to have been a *real* part of.

In charity games, I play in goal. Handling the ball came naturally to me, because of my Rugger

Entertainers often combine their love of football with fund-raising for worthwhile causes. Hence the launching of Goaldiggers', an organisation to provide under-privileged children with football pitches. At the opening of this pitch in Bermondsey, five local kids matched themselves against the 'big boys' – left to right, TV personality David Frost, sports commentator Jimmy Hill, Olympic runner Dave Bedford, actor Tom Courtenay – 'a real enthusiast' says Ed Stewart – and Jimmy Greaves, with (in front) film actor and director Bryan Forbes. Maybe some of these kids will grow to provide the level of professional action personified (right) by Sheffield Wednesday's Brian Joicey, speeding a header through the Hull defence.

Scotland's centre-forward Colin Stein, soon after joining Coventry City.

...thusiast out there on the left wing, and you can realise that if he broke a leg or something, it's possible that a million-pound movie could be badly held up.

In fact, I *did* break my leg in the cause of Soccer. We goalkeepers do take a lot of risks, you know. Ask Gordon Banks, or Peter Shilton, or any of the class men. I'd like to tell you that my leg snapped, just above the right ankle, as I rushed out to make a superb, heart-stopping, sensational save.

I'd like to tell you that, but it just wasn't true. I was running up to take a goal kick, took my eye off the ball for a moment, missed it, awkwardly toppled over ... and by the time the laughter of the fans had died away I knew that my leg had gone and that I'd be in plaster for quite a while.

That very incident, though, made me realise more of the fantastic skills shown by the stars. Pelé, Eusebio, Rodney Marsh, Frannie Lee, George Best ... and, needless to say, each and every member of the Everton first-team squad.

Things change. I can remember when I used to go to football matches, hanging around at the main gate, hoping that one of the star players would smile or say hello. Anything, just to establish a little bit of contact with one of the great men. Now I go to a ground, and the chances are that I'll be surrounded by autograph-seekers. There are so many links between football and show-business.

Funny. I met George Best years back; he was one of the first big-name Soccer men I ever did come face to face with. I wanted to burble out the questions about what his life was like. Instead I could hardly get a word in edgeways as he asked me about whether I ever got scared of drying up on the air and which kind of pop music did I like, and had ever met Lulu or Cilla Black!

Just mark me down as being one of the great Soccer addicts. I'm not quite as bad as Kenny Lynch, a mate of mine ... he won't buy an evening paper if a Soccer recording is due on television, because he can't stand knowing the result before the programme ends!

Going out in front of the loyal Everton fans in that testimonial game meant a great deal to yours truly. I even sampled the Wembley turf and atmosphere once, you know. I conducted the community singing before a big game there. Though I could never have been good enough to actually play there, I know...

background. My team-mates include Bobby Smith, that old England and Spurs goal-getter who still has a shot like a thunderbolt even if there's rather more of him than there was in the Tottenham Cup-and-League double days; and heavyweight boxer of days gone by, Dick Richardson.

But still the love for Everton goes on. I started working in plugs and words of encouragement for the lads even when I joined 'old Auntie' BBC, and in the end the players knew of my support. I still make a train trip to Goodison whenever I can get away from work, and it's fantastic the way the Club makes me feel at home.

Mind you, it's not easy to persuade agents and managers that it is okay for show-business people to take part in sport, even at charity level. You watch someone like Tom Courtenay, a real en-

'Aboard ship, the brightest part of each week was hearing how Everton got on' says fan Ed Stewart. (Right) Everton are getting on pretty well as Tommy Wright tears past Southampton's O'Neil.

now what the players must feel as they come out of that tunnel, into the sunlight, and into an arena where sporting history has so often been made.

Maybe we people in show-business have our pressures – an opening night in a new show, for instance. But I'm ever aware of the pressures that a top-class Soccer player has to go through.

When I play football, it's virtually expected that I'll make a mug of myself, like letting a delicate, tapped-in shot go between my legs. But when Rodney Marsh is through, beating three men on the way, and then 'muffs' his final shot . . . well, that's in the sporting headlines next day as if it was a national disaster.

Though I so desperately wanted to be a sporting star, I think I've probably got the best of both worlds. My sport remains very much my hobby; my job remains very much my way of life. I enjoy both and can generally manage to keep both sides quite separate.

Unless, of course, Everton are going great guns in League or Cup. Then I'm quite likely to share my bias and enthusiasm with as many million people as happen to be listening!

A BIG FISH IN A SMALL POOL, THAT'S BENFICA!

BY JAIME GRACA
of Benfica and Portugal

PORTUGUESE players are often known by nicknames or abbreviations of one of their names but I've been known throughout my career as Jaime Graca. There is a reason for this – that I should be called Jaime Graca rather than 'Jaime', just as many other players are known only by their Christian names.

My football career began with a Club where m elder brother Alfredo played centre-half so right from the start the press and public had to distinguis between the two Graca's. My first club was Vitori Futebol Clube Setubal, a small-town team abou 30 miles from Lisbon.

Even after my transfer to Benfica I continued t live in my birthplace because, with a car, it's almos as easy living there as to move to Lisbon with all i traffic and parking problems. But with Vitoria I wa both lucky and successful. Lucky, because I had a elder brother who had already made it to give m advice and lucky because, playing for an un fashionable team, I was given a chance in th national team.

Otto Gloria, the Brazilian coach who has worke often in Portugal, was in charge of the Portugues team when I got my first cap. Immediately, w were preoccupied with the qualifying matches i the 1966 World Cup. This was a great experienc for me, one of the most satisfying achievements have known in football. Yet, at the same time, bitter disappointment.

I was still with Setubal at the time of the 196 competition, probably unheard of outside Portuga and when the World Cup began I was only 24, wit 7 caps. There were some fine players to help me and everything went like a dream. In the Liverpoo Group, we won all three games, including a 3-1 wi over the World Champions Brazil that almost ever one thought was impossible. I feel sure we made ot of friends in the Liverpool area during that great competition.

Of course, we had a fright in the quarter-finals when we found ourselves three goals down to North Korea. But we had too many good players and too much character to go down easily; we fought back. Mario Coluna and Jose Augusto, who were later to be my Benfica colleagues, were great in those critical games. They kept urging us on, saying we could still win and when Eusebio got first one, then two, of his four goals the whole team began to believe it.

Belief is very important in football and Coluna and Augusto were great believers in good football, which is attacking football, and convinced that allied to hard work you couldn't fail. It is this quality which I think makes Jose Augusto so successful as manager of Portugal's national team now.

After two or three indifferent years Augusto took over in 1971 and within a couple of games he had created a new atmosphere reminiscent of 1966. I was lucky enough to be included again for the Brazilian Independence Cup and we went one better than we did in 1966. At that time we reached the semi-finals and were unlucky enough to be paired with England at Wembley.

England are always a very difficult side to beat but at Wembley everything is doubled. We lost 2-1 in that semi-final though I think ground advantage made all the difference. If for example the game had been played in Lisbon I am sure the result would have gone the other way.

But in Brazil we had a fine spirit and some more very good players, including my Benfica colleague Toni. He is a really outstanding player with all the necessary qualities to take him right to the top. With Eusebio and Simoes recapturing something like their earlier form we did very well in Brazil, playing through the early rounds with ever-growing belief.

Again we met the home country on their own ground – but this time it was in the Final. Brazil were without Pelé but Brazil in Rio de Janeiro is almost as tough a nut as England at Wembley. We nearly made it, too, losing by the only goal of the game scored by Jairzinho in the very last minute. Right until that moment, we were in the game with a real chance. Brazil had more of the play but we never allowed them to get a firm grip on things.

This has been the pattern of my career – being successful to a point but not quite making it at the

More like basketball than football! – Leeds' Peter Lorimer 'imitates the action of the tiger', namely Leicester 'keeper Peter Shilton, as both reach for the ball.

final stages. Since I was transferred to Benfica after the 1966 World Cup we've been Champions of Portugal five times in six seasons and right now we've won our first 19 games 'off the reel', and must surely make it six out of seven.

Though we've often been close we only once reached the European Cup Final. That was of course in 1968 and again, as things turned out, the Final was due to be staged at Wembley and our opponents proved to be England's Manchester United. At that time of course they had George Best and Bobby Charlton at their peak, but we gave as good as we got until extra time.

I had been lucky enough to score an equalising goal for Benfica and we went into extra time hopeful but beginning to feel really tired. You have to play at Wembley and feel the grass gripping your studs, draining the energy out of your muscles, to know what it's really like. Extra time cost us three more goals and we finally lost 1-4.

Since then we have done well in the European Cup but never quite made the top level, though we've been unlucky enough to meet some of the top sides. For example, in the last couple of years we've twice been put out by Ajax though we took them to three games once after winning a fabulous game 3-

n Amsterdam. Another time we lost to Ajax in the emi-finals.

We also met Feyenoord, too, and produced a magnificent performance in Lisbon to beat them ,-1. Our star that day was our young, 20-year-old ight-winger Nene who got three of our goals. He could have a fantastic future, I think.

There is no doubt that Benfica are the outstanding eam in Portugal. They are not only the most successful, but also the wealthiest; they can afford to buy players from other clubs when they get into inancial difficulties. Following me from Setubal wo years ago came their top-scorer, Vitor Baptista, and there's no doubt that Benfica are also the most professional and professionally-organised club in Portugal.

But as we found against Derby, there is a big difference between the game in Portugal and that played in countries like England, where the level of competition is much keener. No team in England or West Germany or Italy, for example, could dominate things as Benfica do in Portugal. There's oo much competition and too many other really professional teams.

This is the problem for the game in Portugal where the standard is good, but not high enough overall. Good football is not enough to be the winners at top level today. You have to be competitive and above all 100 per cent fit, physically and mentally; and battle-hardened. You have to be prepared for a great deal of physical contact, ight marking, and tough tackling.

When we do lose I think it's fair to claim that we go down as good losers and we go down trying to play good football. But in the modern game people only remember the winners and outside Portugal I've never got closer than second best.

Ray Clemence, the Liverpool 'keeper, holds this one from the feet of Wolves' John Richards, with Larry Lloyd beaming on approvingly . . . (Right) Southampton's Bell seems to have the intention of pushing John Craven underground . . . 'I'm a little young for that' might well be Craven's thinking.

SPECIALISTS STILL WANTED EVEN IN TOTAL FOOTBALL

TOTAL Football may well be the 'new reality', but it seems to me that certain heresies are being propagated. There are those who would have us believe that specialisation is dead, that the multi-purpose footballer is king.

No one has more respect for versatility than I have, no one is more delighted to see a centre-half like Georg Schwarzenbeck of West Germany sweeping upfield to initiate and even consummate an attack, or to watch the superbly elegant Franz Beckenbauer now strangling an opposing assault, now accelerating deep into enemy territory. Yet it seems to me there are dangers of over-simplification, that something may well finally be lost.

Take, for example, the question of wing-halves. It was supremely ironical that I should choose to broach the subject with three men who had been splendid Scottish international half-backs them-

Sir Alf Ramsey, the England team manager . . . 'Would we have been overwhelmed by Germany if he had chosen a wing-half?'

The danger is, it seems to me – and one saw it quite exquisitely illustrated on that occasion – that we tend to think purely and simply of 'midfield' players; a breed of cat which, to my mind, just does not exist. The Brazilians make no such mistake. They religiously divide their midfield players into two categories, one approximating to wing-halves, the other to inside-forwards; and surely they, more than anybody, should know what they are about. After all, it was Brazil that gave the world 4-2-4 and 4-3-3, Brazil that, during the Swedish World Cup of 1958, used a half-back and an inside-forward in midfield partnership.

It is also worth noting that when they found that the wing-half in question, the bald, resilient Dino, was rather more of an inside-forward than he should be, rather too far inclined to go surging into attack rather than helping his defence, they replaced him with the more solid Zito. There was no question, of course, of replacing the incomparably poised and inventive Didi.

selves, only minutes before they sent into the field a Manchester United team which was mauled 3-0 at Highbury by Arsenal. All three, that is to say, affirmed and underlined the importance of wing-halves; yet in Manchester United's four man midfield, there wasn't a single recognised half-back.

The three concerned were Matt Busby, Pat Crerand, and Tommy Docherty. Busby, once

BY BRIAN GLANVILLE
Novelist and 'Sunday Times' football writer

captain of Scotland and a splendid, cool half-back with Manchester City and Liverpool, insisted that 'that's where it all starts'. Pat Crerand pointed out, as assistant manager, that all three men in charge at Old Trafford were 'number fours'. Tommy Docherty said that in his day, the chief task of a wing-half was to blot out of the game the opposing inside-forward, that he was forbidden even to cross the half-way line, but he was just as ready to concede the point.

Alan Mullery devastates Wolves in the E.U.F.A Cup Final with this winning goal for Spurs. Mullery himself, says Brian Glanville, was 'demoralised' by being left out of the England side against West Germany. (Right) Tommy Docherty, the Manchester United manager: 'Affirmed and underlined the importance of wing-halves'.

Can it seriously be argued that if Sir Alf Ramsey had picked one genuine wing-half against West Germany in that disastrous European Nations Cup quarter-final in April, 1972, at Wembley, we should have been quite so overwhelmed? Everyone, quite legitimately, expected the choice of opposing the mercurial Gunter Netzer to fall on Alan Mullery, who had played himself so spectacularly back to form, and a place in the Spurs' team. With a piece of what looked like sublime perversity, Ramsey eschewed him, picked a midfield composed wholly of inside-forwards, and allowed Netzer to run wild and inexcusably free.

Mullery, understandably, was demoralised. He did not want, he said, to be considered for England again. The following season, he dropped back into the Second Division, with Fulham. Meanwhile, a born half-back like Mike Bailey of the Wolves continued to give splendid, versatile performances week after week, without coming a step nearer to adding to the solitary cap he won for England in New York against the United States in 1964.

We hear a great deal – far too much – about ball winners, which is too often no more than a euphemism for kickers. No names, no pack drill; and no libel actions. We all know who these rugged gentlemen

The 'L-shaped' game – that's the layout of this shot as Palace centre-half Bell heads away from Southampton centre-forward Gilchrist. (Right) A threatened though accidental 'half nelson' descends on superstar Kevin Keegan of Liverpool as Palace's Mel Blyth beats him in the air.

are. Yet the traditional wing-half was expected to be able to win the ball *and* to use it. Tommy Docherty recalled to me a Swedish half-back who was a ferocious tackler but 'couldn't pass the time of day', so that he was obliged to push the ball unvaryingly to a colleague, standing beside him and ready to distribute.

Yet the great half-backs, such players as Archie Macaulay of Scotland, West Ham, Brentford and Arsenal, Jimmy Scoular of Portsmouth and Newcastle, had a biting tackle; and also the skill, intelligence and artistry to do something original with the ball when they had won it. If you divide your midfield men into the false specialisation of ball winners and distributors, instead of wing-halves and inside-forwards, you are likely to run into the kind of trouble Ramsey encountered against the West Germans, at Wembley.

Then there are the centre-forwards. Not long ago one read a long exegesis, whose object was to per-suade us that there was no longer any such animal, that the breed was dead. This, at the very time that Gerd Muller had almost effortlessly overtaken Uwe Seeler's goal scoring record for West Germany in a matter of a few years! At a time when Giorgio Chinaglia, the tall and powerful Lazio centre forward, had become one of the most highly paid players in the world, thanks to his power, determination and drive – classical qualities of the centre forward.

When, once, I asked Alf Ramsey why there were so few good centre-halves about, he smiled and replied that it was a specialised position; like goalkeeper. Can one seriously disagree with him? Whatever the reasons – and Brian Labone used to think that a centre-half had had much of the ground cut away from beneath his feet by the new double-stopper dispensation – who can deny that centre-halves exist and are horribly hard to find?

Flying tackle from Sheffield United's Trevor Hockey (left) is about to paralyse this run by Birmingham's Campbell. (Facing page) The man whose personality has shone through many a Liverpool and England televised game – Emlyn Hughes.

FOOTBALL AND TV

ATTENDANCES at football matches are tumbling right across Europe and in official quarters, at least, the televising of football is regarded as the big ogre. A handful of people within the game–more aware or perhaps simply more honest–will admit that it is defensive tactics and a general lack of entertainment value that keeps the crowds down. But TV undoubtedly plays some role in the current drift away from the game.

Some officials are pressing for a ban on television cameras at football grounds, suggesting that the game and TV are incompatible. This is not necessarily true, though it should be understood that the priorities of the two bodies put them at odds with each other.

On the one hand are the clubs whose objective is the maximum possible attendances while on the other the desire is to screen not necessarily good football but good television.

There can be no doubt that the televising of matches does affect attendances but it is significant that at the most attractive games the presence of the cameras makes no difference whatsoever. What is required is a rethink of the entire position and a greater degree of willingness from both sides to understand the problems and priorities of the other.

The experience of other countries can be valuable. Austria and Denmark show quite clearly that the public prefers high quality football on TV to watching an inferior product live.

Vienna is in a particularly difficult position. To the north and east are Czechoslovakia and Hungary where each weekend one of the big First Division matches is screened live and in full. The inhabitants of the City are close enough to pick up perfect pictures from both countries on their TV sets. Thus with six First Division clubs in and around the City, the football they present each week must be good or the customers will not come.

With the Austrian game in financial difficulties for some years past and many of the country's best players playing abroad in West Germany and Holland the product offered to the public is too often not as good as that which can be seen in the comfort of one's home free of charge. The only possible answer to the clubs' problem is better, more attractive, football.

In Denmark, too, where the game is still amateur, the standards are not high. During the lengthy winter lay-off Danish TV screens the BBC's 'Match of the Day' every Saturday live at 3 pm, and in full. Later, the TV-watching fans can pick up First Division football screened from East Germany and at 10 pm they can also watch the edited highlights of two matches in West Germany's Bundesliga.

Clearly the Austrians and Danes are in a peculiarly difficult position. They can totally ban any transmissions of their own football but that does not affect the position at all. Ironically enough the Danes appear to be more than willing to watch football if it appeals sufficiently. Why else would 150 fly every Saturday on charter flights from Copenhagen to London specially to watch football?

Facts have to be faced. One of the most unpalatable truths that the football authorities will have to face up to some time is that the game is part of the entertainment industry. If it fails to entertain, then like the cinema and other media the size of the market will shrink.

Each club has its hard core of supporters who will watch their team's home games almost regardless. The people who make up the difference, between the minimum and maximum crowds are the 'floaters'; the people, interested in football, who will go if they think the match will be a good one.

Television, says the Editorial, presents 'only the most interesting and exciting incidents', such as this one, featuring the Liverpool defenders Lindsay and Lloyd, squeezing out in the air Palace's John Craven. (Facing page) The man who almost certainly will be dominating those World Cup pictures on your screen – West Germany's Gerd Muller.

When playing standards decline or if the level of entertainment drops because, as now, the game is going through a period of defensive thinking, these floating spectators stay at home and satisfy themselves with what they see on television.

The football answer to the problem of falling gates is therefore to be more enterprising. Accept the fact that each year only one club can win the Championship and only two teams can play in the FA Cup Final. But they can all attempt to play attractive, attacking football, encouraging skill and flair, seeking to score goals rather than to prevent them. This, in the final analysis, is the only way to bring in good crowds consistently.

Everyone can entertain and give value for money—if the will is there.

Television should adapt its approach, too. At present they show edited highlights, presenting to the viewers only the most interesting and exciting incidents from a match. Thus they give a distorted picture, suggesting that live football is full of goal-mouth incidents, goals, and shots which rebound from the framework of the goal or are brilliantly saved.

Football programmes on television should take a broader view and seek to inform and educate the public about the intricacies of the game and its

finer points. There should also be an attempt made to bring onto the screen for interviews, people who really have something interesting and informative to say about the game rather than, as now, show the same old faces simply because they have talented feet or are managers of successful clubs.

There is also a need for a broad-based, magazine-type football programme which should be truly international. Star players from abroad could be featured showing not only how they play but how they live and spend their leisure time. Big names need not necessarily be barred but they should be selected not on their reputations or their profiles but on what they can contribute to the programme and the game of football.

Above all, the football authorities should rethink their position on re-runs of controversial incidents. At present it appears they would like a total ban on re-runs of incidents in which the referees appear to have made errors. And it seems that part of the TV deal is that foul play and unsporting incidents should be deleted from the film before screening.

On both these points there should be a fresh approach. Let the authorities do something constructive that will raise the standards of refereeing and let the clubs discourage foul play and unsporting behaviour.

Right at the heart of the current gates' crisis is the firmly-held belief that winning is everything. Until that is changed, until it is appreciated that football should be skilful and entertaining, as well as exciting, the crowds will sink lower before they get bigger.

Juventus inside-forward Bettega finished top scorer in his Club's Italian Championship season even though out half the season with a chest infection. Now recovered, he's expected to be a 'main man' in Italy's World Cup effort.

THE YEAR'S INTERNATIONAL FOOTBALL

THE year – so far as international football was concerned – belonged to Europe. That is really no more than one should expect, with almost 12 million of the world's total of 15.6 million registered players living and playing in Europe. And of the European footballing nations pride of place must go to the West Germans for their wholly convincing triumph in the European Football Championship.

Our survey last year ended with the qualifying competition for the championship. The quarter finals were played on the 29/30 April (first legs) and the 13/14 May (second legs). Three of the first legs were drawn, with the matches between Yugoslavia and the Soviet Union in Belgrade, and between Italy and Belgium in Milan both goalless, and Hungary and Rumania sharing two goals in Budapest. The Soviet Union, with a very good record in the competition since its inception as the Nations Cup in 1960, had been expected to beat Yugoslavia and duly did so by three goals to nil when the second leg was played in Moscow.

Belgium and Rumania, on the other hand, had upset 'form' calculations by gaining a point apiece, and Belgium were able to benefit from home advantage in Brussels in the second leg when they beat Italy 2–1. Rumania were not so successful. It was the Hungarians who scored first, through Szoke, in the second leg in Bucharest. Dobrin equalised but Kocsis had restored Hungary's lead before the interval. Nine minutes from time Neagu delighted the 100,000 crowd by equalising for the home country but the Rumanians were unable to clinch victory. The deciding match was played three days later in Belgrade – and was watched by a good crowd of 32,130. It was again a close thing with Szoke only scoring Hungary's second goal in their odd goal in three victory just one minute from time.

So, three of the semi-finalists were the Soviet Union, Belgium and Hungary. The fourth was West Germany – thanks effectively to their 3–1 win over England at Wembley in the first leg.

The matches between England and Germany have always seemed to have a significance beyond the game itself. From 1908 England had played international matches in Vienna, Budapest and Prague against Austria, Hungary and Bohemia but England had not played against Germany before the outbreak of the First World War in 1914. After that war the British associations were opposed to the early resumption of relationship with the ex-enemy countries and, indeed, made their first break from FIFA on that issue. It was not until 1930 that the first match was played between England and Germany. The venue was Berlin and six goals were shared. Five years passed before the return fixture. Hitler was in power but had not yet made sport part of the Nazi propaganda machine. England won the match at Tottenham by three goals to nil.

The situation had changed by May 1938 when England were due to play again in Berlin. Hitler – taking his cue in this respect from Mussolini – regarded any success by German sportsmen, and sportswomen, as evidence of the supremacy of his master German race. Nor was the considerable opposition in Britain to the idea of England playing the match in Berlin modified by the way in which the Nazis had marched in and annexed Austria two months before. That had been enough to persuade Cabinet ministers to cry enough and resign from the Government. The plea that politics should not interfere with sport advanced in favour of fulfilling the fixture was scarcely maintained when the England players, lined up before the kick-off in the Olympic Stadium, Berlin, were instructed to give the Nazi salute! On the field, however, the players gave their answer with a notable 6–3 victory.

After the Second World War there was less delay in resuming sporting relations with ex-enemy countries and the West Germans came to Wembley in December 1954. Then, and in the return match in Berlin in May 1956, England won 3–1. The next two matches, in Nuremberg in May 1965 and at Wembley in February 1966, also had the same result – an England victory by one goal to nil. So to the World Cup Final of July 1966 with the record between the two standing at 7 matches played; 6 England wins and one match drawn. England, as every schoolboy knows, won by four goals to two – and the Germans might have been forgiven for believing that they would never beat England. Instead they have since gone a long way towards balancing the score!

The German 'revenge' began in June 1968 when England played a friendly at Hanover en route to

Italy for the final stages of the European Football Championship for which England had qualified along with Italy, Yugoslavia and the Soviet Union. The match in Hanover was not a particularly good one but it was ominous that the only goal of the match was scored in the last ten minutes when a speculative, down-the-middle shot from Beckenbauer was deflected with Gordon Banks moving the wrong way (the right way had it not been for the deflection!). Four days later England lost their EFC semi-final against Yugoslavia again by the only goal of the match scored four minutes from time. The England–West Germany paths crossed again in the quarter-final of the 1970 World Cup in Leon. With just over twenty minutes left to play England held the two-goal lead they had established soon after the interval. Then the Germans pulled level and, unlike four years before at Wembley, it was the Germans who won in extra time.

Then fate – in the shape of the draw for the quarter finals of the 1972 EFC – brought England and West Germany together again. The West Germans had spluttered a bit in the qualifying competition – dropping points at home in drawn matches with Poland and Albania and only beating the latter by a single goal in Tirana. But, like England, they had won all three of their away matches. And the West Germans had to play the first leg against England away – at Wembley where they had been beaten on their three previous visits.

It was different for them last year on 29 April. Maybe a month later the result would have been different since the match was played when Derby, Leeds, Liverpool and Manchester City were involved in a cliffhanger finish for the Football League Championship, and played a week before Arsenal and Leeds were to meet in the FA Cup Final. Anything more than a cursory get-together before the match was not possible for the England players. Still with five minutes to go it looked as if the match would end one-all. Then Bobby Moore of all people conceded a needless penalty and although Banks got to Netzer's shot from the spot he could only push the ball onto the upright and then watch it go into the goal; and finally in the last minute an ill-judged back pass gave Gerd Muller the sort of chance that he never scorns to take. A goalless match in the second leg a fortnight later whilst it slotted into England's sequence of undefeated away matches

from Leon to date did not disturb the German overall superiority.

Now it is for England to assert their old mastery and, of course, the chance seemed likely to come in the 1974 World Cup final tournament to be staged in West Germany. Instead by only drawing at home against Wales in the qualifying competition England, at the time of writing, have made their task of qualifying more difficult. Poland, the third country in the group, may also drop points against Wales–hitherto the Poles have not been good travellers, but England's certain way to qualify will be to beat Poland twice.

Not that England are the only fancied finalists to have dropped unexpected points–Italy were held to a draw at home by Turkey, for example. The results to date and the programme for the qualifying competition are set out for you after the line-ups. So far as this year's line-ups are concerned I have concentrated on the Europeans and in particular some of those involved with the British countries and the Republic of Ireland in their qualifying groups. The year (1972) saw Brazil's Independence Cup tournament in which a number of European countries took part–including the Soviet Union who were, however, mainly represented by players of the Zaria Voroshilovgrad club whose league fixtures were suspended for the period–but who nevertheless won the Soviet championship, and representative elevens drawn from the Central and North American Confederation (CONCACAF) and from Africa. France played both and for interest I have included the French line-ups although these cannot count as inter-*national* matches. Also contested in 1972 were the final stages of the Olympic Football Tournament–the standing of the matches are a puzzle for statisticians but I have worked on the principle that where, as in the Soviet countries and others like Denmark, there is no recognised professional structure Olympic matches between national teams must be counted as Full internationals.

GORDON JEFFERY

Legend: Unless otherwise indicated the line-ups are in 4–3–3 formation. Olymp–Olympic matches; EFC–European Football Championship; WC–World Cup qualifying; BHC–British Home Championship

WEST GERMANY

A 29. 3. 72 Hungary............0 West Germany.......2 — Budapest
(Breitner, Hoeness)

B 29. 4. 72 England............1 West Germany.......3 — Wembley (EFC)
(Lee) (Hoeness, Netzer, Muller)

C 13. 5. 72 West Germany......0 England............0 — West Berlin (EFC)

D 26. 5. 72 West Germany......4 U.S.S.R............1 — Munich
(Muller 4) (Kolotov)

E 14. 6. 72 Belgium...........1 West Germany.......2 — Antwerp (EFC)
(Polleunis) (Muller 2)

F 18. 6. 72 West Germany......3 U.S.S.R............0 — Brussels (EFC FINAL)
(Muller 2, Wimmer)

G 15. 11. 72 West Germany......5 Switzerland.........1 — Dusseldorf
(Muller 4, Netzer) (Kunzli)

H 14. 2. 73 West Germany......2 Argentina..........3 — Munich
(Heynckes, Cullmann (Ghio, Alonso, Brindisi)

	A	B	C	D	E	F	G	H
Maier..........	G	G	G	G[1]	G	G	G	G
Kleff..........	—	—	G[2]	—	—	—	—	—
Hottges........	RB	RB	RB	RB[1]	RB	RB	RB	LB
Bonhof.........	—	—	—	RB[2]	—	—	—	—
Beckenbauer.....	RCB	RCB	RCB	RCB	RCB	RCB	RCB	RCB
Schwarzenbeck...	LCB	LCB	LCB	LCB	LCB	LCB	LCB	LCB[1]
Breitner........	LB	LB	LB	LB	LB	LB	LB	LH
Wimmer........	RH	RH	LH	LH	LH	LH	LH[1]	RH
Flohe..........	CH	—	RH					
Hoeness........	RF	CH	RF[1]	RH	RH[1]	RH	RH	—
Netzer.........	LH	LH	CH	CH	CH	CH	CH	
Overath........	—	—	—	—	—	—		CH
Vogts..........	—	—	—	—	—	—	LH[2]	RB
Grabowski.......	—	RF		—	RH[2]			
Heynckes.......	LF[1]	—	RF[2]	RF	RF	RF	RF	CF
Muller.........	CF	CF	CF	CF	CF	CF	CF	
Held..........	LF[2]	LF	LF					LF[2]
Kremers........	—	—		LF	LF	LF	LF[1]	LF[1]
Geye..........	—	—					LF[2]	RF
Cullmann.......	—						—	LCB[2]

AUSTRIA

A 8. 4. 72 Czechoslovakia.......2 Austria.............0 — Brno
(Petras, Ternenyi)

B 30. 4. 72 Austria.............4 Malta..............0 — Vienna (WC)
(Hickersberger 3, Hof)

C 10. 6. 72 Austria.............2 Sweden.............0 — Vienna (WC)
(Parits, Pumm)

D 3. 9. 72 Rumania...........1 Austria.............1 — Craiova
(Dembrovski) (Hickersberger)

E 15. 10. 72 Austria.............2 Hungary...........2 — Vienna (WC)
(Hasil, Jara) (Dunai II, Kocsis)

F 26. 11. 72 Malta..............0 Austria.............2 — Valetta (WC)
(Kogelberger, Spitzeri o.g.)

	A*	B	C	D	E	F			A*	B	C	D	E	F
Rettensteiner.....	G	—	—	—	—	—		Daxbacher.......	—	RH	—	—	—	—
Stachowicz......	—	G	—	—	G	G		Hasil	—	—	RH	—	CH	—
Koncilia........	—	—	G	—	—	—		Hickersberger....	LH	RF	RF	RF	RH	RH
Fuchsbichler.....	—	—	—	G	—	—		Ettmayer........	LCH	—	LH[1]	—	—	—
Sara...........	RB[1]	—	—	RB	—	RB		Hof...........	—	LH	CH[1]	—	—	LCB[2]
Stengler........	RB[2]	—	—	—	—	—		Starek.........	—	—	LH[2]	LH	LH	CH
Schmid-Radner ..	RH	RB	—	LCB	LCB	RCB		Gallos.........	—	—	—	—	—	LH
Pumm	LB	—	RB	RH	RB	LB		Kreuz.........	RF	CH				
Sturmberger.....	RCB	RCB	RCB					Kogelberger	—	—		CF	RF	RF
Horvath........	RCH	LCB	LCB	RCB	RCB	—		Hattenberger.....	—	—	CH[2]	CH	—	—
Eigenstiller	LCB	LB	LB	—	LB	LCB[1]		Parits.........	—	CF	CF	—	CF	CF
Krieger	—	—	—	LB	—	—		Jara	LF	LF	LF	LF	LF	LF

*4 + 2

135

ENGLAND

A 29. 4. 72 England............1 West Germany.......3 — Wembley (EFC)
      (Lee)   (Hoeness, Netzer, Muller)

B 13. 5. 72 West Germany.......0 England............0 — West Berlin (EFC)

C 20. 5. 72 Wales..............0 England............3 — Cardiff (BHC)
                                     (Hughes, Marsh, Bell)

D 23. 5. 72 England............0 N. Ireland..........1 — Wembley (BHC)
                                     (Neill)

E 27. 5. 72 Scotland...........0 England............1 — Glasgow (BHC)
                                     (Ball)

F 11. 10. 72 England............1 Yugoslavia..........1 — Wembley
      (Royle)   (Vladic)

G 15. 11. 72 Wales..............0 England............1 — Cardiff (WC)
                                     (Bell)

H 24. 1. 73 England............1 Wales..............1 — Wembley (WC)
      (Hunter)   (Toshack)

I 14. 2. 73 Scotland...........0 England............5 — Glasgow
                        (Lorimer o.g., Clarke 2, Channon, Chivers)

	A	B	C	D	E	F	G	H	I
Banks	G	G	G	—	G	—	—	—	—
Shilton	—	—	—	G	—	G	—	—	G
Clemence	—	—	—	—	—	—	G	G	—
Madeley	RB	RB	RB	—	RB	—	—	—	RCB
Todd	—	—	—	RB	—	—	—	—	—
Mills	—	—	—	—	—	RB	—	—	—
Storey	—	RH	RH	RH	RH	RH	RB	RB	RB
McFarland	—	RCB	RCB	—	RCB	—	RCB	RCB	—
Lloyd	—	—	—	RCB	—	—	—	—	—
Blockley	—	—	—	—	—	RCB	—	—	—
Hunter	LCB	LH[1]	LH	LCB	LH	—	LH	LH	—
Moore	RCB	LCB	LCB	—	LCB	LCB	LCB	LCB	LCB
Hughes	LB	LB	LB	LB	LB	—	LB	LB	LB
Lampard	—	—	—	—	—	LB	—	—	—
Bell	RH	RF	CH	CH	CH	LH	RH	RH	RH
Ball	CH	CH	—	RF	CH	CH	CH	CH	CH
Peters	LH	LH[2]	—	LH[2]	—	—	—	—	LH
Currie	—	—	—	LH[1]	—	—	—	—	—
Lee	RF	—	—	—	—	—	—	—	—
Summerbee	—	LF[2]	RF	RF	—	—	—	—	—
Channon	—	—	—	—	—	RF	—	—	RF
Keegan	—	—	—	—	—	—	RF	RF	—
Chivers	CF	CF	—	CF[2]	CF	—	CF	CF	CF
Macdonald	—	—	CF	CF[1]	LF[2]	—	—	—	—
Royle	—	—	—	—	—	CF	—	—	—
Hurst	LF[1]	—	—	—	—	—	—	—	—
Marsh	LF[2]	LF[1]	LF	LF	LF[1]	LF	LF	LF	—
Clarke	—	—	—	—	—	—	—	—	LF

WALES

A 20. 5. 72 Wales..............0 England............3 — Cardiff (BHC)
                                   (Hughes, Marsh, Bell)

B 24. 5. 72 Scotland...........1 Wales..............0 — Glasgow (BC)
                        (Lorimer)

C 27. 5. 72 Wales..............0 N. Ireland..........0 — Wrexham (BHC)

D 15. 11. 72 Wales..............0 England............1 — Cardiff (WC)
                                     (Bell)

E 24. 1. 73 England............1 Wales..............1 — Wembley (WC)
      (Hunter)   (Toshack)

	A	B	C	D	E
Sprake	G	G	G	G	G
Rodrigues	RB	—	LH[2]	RB[1]	RB[1]
Page	—	RB	RB	—	RB[2]
England	RCB	LCB	RCB	LCB	RCB
Hennessey	RH	RCB[1]	—	RCB	—
Roberts	LCB[1]	—	LCB	—	LCB
Thomas	LB	LB	LB	LB	LB
Phillips	—	RH	RH	RH	—
Durban	CH	CH	CH	—	—

	A	B	C	D	E
Hockey	—	—	—	CH	CH
Yorath	LH	LH	LH[1]	—	RH
Mahoney	—	—	—	LH	LH
Wyn Davies	RF	RF	RF	RF	—
James	—	RCB[2]	—	LF	RF
Ron Davies	CF	CF	CF	—	—
Toshack	LF	—	—	CF	CF
Reece	LCB[2]	LF	LF	RB[2]	—
B. Evans	—	—	—	—	LF

NETHERLANDS

A	16. 2. 72	Greece.............0	Netherlands.........5	— Athens	
		(Hulshoff 2, Cruyff 2, Neeskens)			
B	3. 5. 72	Netherlands.........3	Peru...............0	— Rotterdam	
		(Klijnjan, Van Hanegem, Schneider)			
C	30. 8. 72	Czechoslovakia.......1 (Hagara)	Netherlands.........2 (Cruyff, Neeskens)	— Prague	
D	1. 11. 72	Netherlands.........9 (Neeskens 3, Cruyff 2, De Jong, Broekamp 2, Keizer)	Norway............0	— Rotterdam (WC)	
E	19. 11. 72	Belgium.............0	Netherlands.........0	— Rotterdam (WC)	

	A*	B	C	D	E*
van Beveren	G	G	G	G	G
Venneker	RB	—	—	—	—
Schneider	—	RB	RB	RB	—
Mansveld	—	—	RCB	RCB	RB
Israel	RCB	RCB	—	—	—
Hulshoff	LCB	LCB	LCB	LCB	RCB
Krol	LB	LB	LB	LB	LCB
Suurbier	—	—	—	—	LB
Neeskens	RH	—	CH	CH	LH
Jansen	—	RH	—	—	—

	A*	B	C	D	E*
De Jong	OR	—	RH	RH	RH
van Hanegem	LH	CH	LH¹	LH	LCF
Klijnjan	—	LH	—	—	—
Haan	—	—	—	LH²	—
Wery	RCF	RF	—	—	—
Swart	—	—	RF	—	—
Broekamp	—	—	—	RF²	OR
Cruyff	LCF	CF	CF	CF	RCF
Kiezer	OL	LF¹	—	LF	OL
Muhren	—	LF²	—	—	—
Pahlplatz	—	—	LF	RF¹	—

*4–2–4

POLAND

A	16. 4. 72	Bulgaria............3 (Bonev 2, Dermendjiev)	Poland..............1 (Lubanski)	— Stara Zagora (Olym)	
B	7. 5. 72	Poland..............3 (Banas 2, Marks)	Bulgaria............0	— Warsaw (Olym)	
C	10. 5. 72	Poland..............0	Switzerland.........0	— Poznan	
D	1. 9. 72	Poland..............2 (Gorgon 2)	East Germany........1 (Streich)	— Nuremberg (WG) (Olym)	
E	3. 9. 72	Poland..............1 (Deyna)	Denmark.............1 (Avro Hansen)	— Regensburg (WG) (Olym)	
F	5. 9. 72	Poland..............2 (Deyna, Szoltysik)	U.S.S.R.............1 (Blochin)	— Augsburg (WG) (Olym)	
G	10. 9. 72	Poland..............2 (Deyna 2)	Hungary.............1 (Varadi)	— Munich (WG) (Olympic FINAL)	
H	15. 10. 72	Poland..............3 (Deyna 2, Gadocha)	Czechoslovakia.......0	— Bydgoszcz	

	A	B	C	D*	E	F*	G*	H*
Kostka	G	G	G¹	G	G	G	G	G
Szeja	—	—	G²	—	—	—	—	—
Szymanowski	RB	—	RB	RB	RB	RB	—	—
Wrazy	LCB	RB	—	—	—	—	—	—
Gut	—	—	—	RH	RH²	RH¹	RB	RB
Ostafinski	RCB	—	—	LCB¹	—	RCB	—	—
Gorgon	—	RCB	RCB¹	RCB	RCB	LCB¹	RCB	RCB
Cmikiewicz	—	LCB	LCB	RCH	LCB	RCH	LCB	LCB
Pazdzior	—	—	LCB	—	—	—	—	—
Anczok	LB	LB	—	LB	LB	LB	LB	—
Musial	—	—	LB	—	—	—	—	LB
Kraska	—	RH	—	LH	LH	—	LCB²	RCH	RCH
Szoltysik	LH	RH	—	—	RH¹	RH²	RH	RH
Polak	—	LH²	RH	—	—	—	—	—
Deyna	CH	CH	CH	LCH	CH	LCH	LCH¹	LCH
Maszczyk	—	LH¹	RCB²	—	LH	LH	LH	LH
Syzmczak	—	—	LCB²	—	—	—	LCH²	—
Banas	RF¹	RF	—	—	—	—	—	—
Marks	LF²	LF²	RF¹	—	RF¹	—	—	—
Nowak	—	—	RF²	—	—	—	—	—
Lubanski	CF	CF	CF	RF	CF	RF	RF	—
Wojciechowski	—	—	—	—	—	—	—	RF
Gadocha	RF²	LF¹	LF	LF	LF	LF	LF	LF
Jarosik	LF¹	—	—	—	—	—	—	—
Lato	—	—	—	—	RF²	—	—	—

*4–4–2

FRANCE

A 8. 4. 72 Rumania...........2 France..............0 — Bucharest
 (Iordanescu, Dinu)
B 11. 6. 72 France..............5 Concacaf XI.........0 — Salvador (Brazil)
 (Bereta, Revelli 3,
 Bulnes o.g.)
C 15. 6. 72 France..............2 Africa XI...........0 — Maceio (Brazil)
 (Blanchet, Floch)
D 18. 6. 72 France..............3 Colombia...........2 — Salvador (Brazil)
 (Loubet, Molitor,   (Pinheiro, Mesa)
 Larque)
E 25. 6. 72 France..............0 Argentina...........0 — Salvador (Brazil)
F 3. 9. 72 Greece..............1 France..............3 — Athens
 (Sarafis)   (Michel, H. Revelli, Larque)
G 13. 10. 72 France..............1 U.S.S.R.............0 — Paris (WC)
 (Bereta)
H 15. 11. 72 Rep. of Ireland......2 France..............1 — Dublin (WC)
 (Conroy, Treacy)   (Larque)

	A*	B*	C*	D*	E*	F*	G*	H*
Carnus	G	—	—	G	G	G	G	G
Baratelli	—	G	G	—	—	—	—	—
Tresor	RB	LCB	LCB¹	RCB	LCB	LB	LCB	LCB
Djorkaeff	—	RB	RB	RB	RB	RB¹	—	—
Broissart	—	—	—	—	—	RB²	RB	RB
Novi	RCB	—	—	—	RCB	—	—	—
Quittet	LH²	RCB	RCB	LCB	—	LCB	RCB	RCB
Adams	—	—	LCB²	LH	RCB	RH	LH	RH
Bosquier	LCB	—	—	—	—	—	—	—
Rostagni	LB	LB	LB	—	LB	—	LB	LB
Jodar	—	—	—	LB	—	—	—	—
Michel	RH	RH	RH	RH	RH	LH	RH	—
Mezy	LH¹	LH	LH	—	LH	—	—	—
Huck	—	—	—	—	—	—	—	LH
Blanchet	OR	OR¹	OR	—	OR	—	—	—
Floch	RCF¹	OR²	OL²	OR¹	—	—	—	—
Lech	LCF	LCF²	LCF	RCF²	LCF	OR¹	—	—
Chiesa	—	—	—	—	—	—	OR¹	—
Loubet	—	—	—	OL	—	OR²	OR²	OR¹
Molitor	RCF²	—	—	RCF¹	—	—	—	OR²
Revelli	—	RCF	RCF	—	RCF	RCF	RCF	RCF
Larque	OL²	LCF¹	—	LCF	—	LCF	LCF	LCF
Bereta	OL¹	OL	OL¹	OR²	OL	OL	OL	OL

*4-2-4

NORTHERN IRELAND

A 16. 2. 72 Northern Ireland.....1 Spain...............1 — Hull (EFC)
 (Morgan)   (Rojo)
B 20. 5. 72 Scotland...........2 Northern Ireland.....0 — Glasgow (BHC)
 (Law, Lorimer)
C 23. 5. 72 England.............0 Northern Ireland.....1 — Wembley (BHC)
   (Neill)
D 27. 5. 72 Wales..............0 Northern Ireland.....0 — Wrexham (BHC)
E 18. 10. 72 Bulgaria............3 Northern Ireland.....0 — Sofia (WC)
 (Bonev 2, Kolev)
F 14. 2. 73 Cyprus.............1 Northern Ireland.....0 — Nicosia (WC)
 (Antoniou)

	A	B	C	D	E	F*			A	B	C	D	E	F*
Jennings	G	G	G	G	G	G		McMordie	LH	RF¹	RF	RF	LF	—
Rice	RB	RB	RB	RB	RB	RB		Jackson	—	LH	LH	LH	—	—
Neill	RCB	RCB	RCB	RCB	RCB	RCB		Morgan	RF	—	—	—	RH²	—
Hunter	LCB	LCB	LCB	LCB	LCB	LCB		Best	CF	—	—	—	RF	—
Nelson	LB	LB	LB	LB	LB	LB		Dougan	—	CF	CF	CF¹	CF	LCF
Hamilton	RH¹	—	—	—	RH¹	OR		McIlroy	LF	RF²	CF²	—	—	—
Hegan	—	RH	RH	RH	LH	RH		Irvine	—	LF	LF	LF	—	—
Clements	CH	CH¹	CH	CH	CH	LH		O'Neill	RH²	—	—	CF²	—	—
Craig	—	CH²	—	—	—	LB		Dickson	—	—	—	—	—	RCF

*4-2-4

HUNGARY

A 12. 1. 72 Spain 1   Hungary .... 0 — Madrid
(Arieta)

B 29. 3. 72 Hungary 0   West Germany .... 2 — Budapest
(Breitner, Hoeness)

C 29. 4. 72 Hungary 1   Rumania .... 1 — Budapest (EFC)
(Branikovitz) (Satmareanu)

D 6. 5. 72 Hungary 3   Malta .... 0 — Budapest (WC)
(Kocsis, Bene, I. Juhasz)

E 14. 5. 72 Rumania 2   Hungary .... 2 — Bucharest (EFC)
(Dobrin, Neagu) (Szoke, Kocsis)

F 17. 5. 72 Hungary 2   Rumania .... 1 — Belgrade (Yugo) (EFC)
(Kocsis, Szoke) (Neagu)

G 25. 5. 72 Sweden 0   Hungary .... 0 — Stockholm (WC)

H 14. 6. 72 U.S.S.R. 1   Hungary .... 0 — Brussels (Belg) (EFC)
(Konkov)

I 17. 6. 72 Belgium 2   Hungary .... 1 — Liege (EFC)
(Lambert, Van Himst) (Ku)

J 31. 8. 72 Hungary 2   Denmark .... 0 — Augsburg (WG) (Olym)
(Ede Dunai 2)

K 3. 9. 72 Hungary 2   East Germany .... 0 — Passau (WG) (Olym)
(A. Dunai, Toth)

L 10. 9. 72 Poland 2   Hungary .... 1 — Munich (WG) (Olym FINAL)
(Deyna 2) (Varadi)

M 15. 10. 72 Austria 2   Hungary .... 2 — Vienna (WC)
(Hasil, Jara) (A. Dunai, Kocsis)

	A	B	C	D*	E	F	G	H	I	J	K*	L	M
Geczi	G	—	G	G	G	—	G	G	G	G	G	G	G
Rothermel	—	G	—	—	—	G	—	—	—	—	—	—	—
Fabian	RB	—	RB	—	RB	RB	RB	RB	RB	—	—	—	—
Pancsics	—	RB	RCB	RCB	RCB	RCB	RCB	RCB	RCB	RCB	RCB	RCB	RB
Vepi	—	—	LB	RB	—	—	—	—	—	RB	RB	RB	—
Kovacs	RCB	RCB	—	—	—	—	—	—	—	—	—	—	RCB
P. Juhasz	LCB	LB	—	LB	LB	LB	LB	LB	LB	LB	LB	LB	LB
Balint	—	LCB	LCB	—	LCB	LCB	LCB	LCB	LCB	LCB	LCB	LCB	LCB
Vidats	LB	CH	—	LCB	—	—	—	—	—	—	—	—	—
Szucs	RH	RH	CH	LH	LH	CH[1]	RH	—	LF[2]	RH	RH	RH	CH
Kocsis	—	—	RH[1]	LCF[2]	CH[1]	LH	CH	CH[1]	—	LF[1]	OL[1]	CH[2]	LH
I. Juhasz	LH[1]	—	—	RH	RH	RH	—	RH	RH	—	—	—	RH
Fazekas	CH	LH	LH	—	—	—	—	—	—	—	—	—	—
Ku	—	—	—	—	CH[2]	CH[2]	LH	LH	LH	LF[2]	OL[2]	CH[1]	—
Albert	—	—	—	—	—	—	—	CH[2]	CH	—	—	—	—
Kozma	—	—	—	—	—	—	—	RF	CH[1]	—	—	—	—
K. Toth	—	—	—	—	—	—	—	—	—	CH[2]	OR	RF[2]	—
Szalai	LH[2]	—	—	—	—	—	—	—	—	—	—	—	—
Varadi	—	—	—	—	—	—	—	—	—	LH	LH[1]	LF	—
Bene	RF	RF[2]	RH[2]	RCF	CF	CF	CF	CF[1]	—	—	—	—	—
Branikovitz	—	RF[1]	RF	—	—	—	—	—	—	—	LH[2]	—	—
Szoke	CF[2]	—	—	OR	RF[1]	RF	RF[1]	RF	—	—	—	—	RF[1]
A. Dunai II	CF[1]	CF	CF	LCF[1]	RF[2]	LF	RF[2]	CF[2]	CF	RF	RCF	RF[1]	CF
E. Dunai III	—	—	—	—	—	—	—	—	—	CF	LCF	LH	—
Zambo	LF	LF	LF	OL	LF	—	LF	LF	LF[1]	—	—	—	LF

*4–2–4

PORTUGAL

A	29. 3. 72	Portugal...........4 (Humberto, Nene, Jorge, Jordao)		Cyprus.............o	—	Lisbon (WC)	
B	10. 5. 72	Cyprus.............o		Portugal............1 (Chico)	—	Nicosia (WC)	
C	11. 6. 72	Portugal...........3 (Eusebio, Dinis, Nene)		Ecuador............o	—	Natal (Brazil)	
D	14. 6. 72	Portugal...........3 (Eusebio, Dinis, Toni)		Iran...............o	—	Recife (Brazil)	
E	18. 6. 72	Portugal...........4 (Humberto, Dinis 2, Eusebio)		Chile..............1 (Crisoto)	—	Recife (Brazil)	
F	25. 6. 72	Portugal...........2 (Peres, Nene)		Rep. of Ireland.......1 (Leech)	—	Recife (Brazil)	
G	29. 6. 72	Portugal...........3 (Adolfo, Dinis, Eusebio)		Argentina...........1	—	Rio (Brazil)	
H	2. 7. 72	Portugal...........1 (Peres)		Uruguay............1 (Pavoni)	—	Rio (Brazil)	
I	6. 7. 72	Portugal...........1 (Jordao)		U.S.S.R............o	—	Belo Horizonte (Brazil)	
J	9. 7. 72	Brazil.............1 (Jaizinho)		Portugal............o	—	Rio	

	A	B	C*	D*	E*	F*	G*	H*	I*	J
Henrique........	G	G	G	G	G	G	G	G	G	G
Rebello.........	RB	—	—	—	—	—	—	—	—	—
Artur...........	—	RB	RB	RB	RB	RB	RB	RB	RB	RB
Humberto.......	RCB	RCB	RCB	RCB	RCB	RCB	RCB	RCB	RCB	RCB
Rolando........	LCB	—	—	—	—	—	—	—	—	—
Freitas.........	—	LCB	—	—	—	—	—	—	—	—
Loranjeira.......	—	—	LCB	—	—	—	—	—	—	—
Messias.........	—	—	—	LCB	LCB	LCB	LCB	LCB	LCB	LCB
Carrico........	LB	—	—	—	—	—	—	—	—	—
Matine..........	—	LB	LH²	LH	LH²	—	—	—	—	—
Adolfo..........	—	—	LB	LB	LB	LB	LB	LB	LB	LB
Graca..........	RH	RH	LH¹	—	LH¹	LH	LH	LH	LH	LH
Toni...........	LH	LH	RH	RH	RH	RH	RH	RH	RH	CH
Eusebio........	CH¹	—	LCF	LCF	LCF	LCF	LCF	LCF	LCF	CF
Peres..........	CH²	LF	RCF	OR¹	RCF¹	RCF	RCF	RCF	OR	RH
Chico..........	—	CH	—	—	—	—	—	—	—	—
Nene..........	RF¹	—	OR²	—	—	OL²	—	—	OL²	—
Dinis..........	RF²	CF²	OR¹	OR²	OR	OR	OR	OR	RCF¹	RF
Jorge..........	CF	RF¹	—	RCF	RCF²	—	—	—	RCF²	LF²
Abel...........	—	RF²	—	—	—	—	—	—	—	—
Battista........	—	CF¹	—	—	—	—	—	—	—	—
Jordao........	LF	—	OL	OL	OL	OL¹	OL	OL	OL¹	LF¹

*4-2-4

CZECHOSLOVAKIA

A	8. 4. 72	Czechoslovakia......2 (Petras, Ternenyi)	Austria..............o	—	Brno	
B	26. 4. 72	Czechoslovakia......6 (Jan Capkovic 2, Jokl, Kuna 2, Dobias)	Luxembourg.........o	—	Pilsen	
C	14. 5. 72	Sweden.............1 (Hult)	Czechoslovakia.......2 (Jokl 2)	—	Gothenburg	
D	28. 6. 72	Brazil.............o	Czechoslovakia.......o	—	Rio	
E	2. 7. 72	Czechoslovakia......o	Scotland............o	—	Porto Alegre (Brazil)	
F	6. 7. 72	Yugoslavia.........2 (Bajevic, Dzajic)	Czechoslovakia.......1 (Hrusecky)	—	Sao Paulo (Brazil)	
G	30. 8. 72	Czechoslovakia......1 (Hagara)	Netherlands.........2 (Cruyff, Neeskens)	—	Prague	
H	15. 10. 72	Poland.............3 (Deyna 2, Gadocha)	Czechoslovakia.......o	—	Bydgoszcz	
I	1. 11. 72	Czechoslovakia......1 (Pekarik)	East Germany........3 (Kreische 2, P. Ducke)	—	Bratislava	

—Qualifying Competition—

Group I

	Aus.	Hun.	Mal.	Swe.	P	W	D	L	F	A	Pts.
Austria	—	2-2	4-0	2-0	4	3	1	0	10	2	7
Hungary		—	3-0		4	2	2	0	7	2	6
Malta	0-2	0-2	—		5	0	0	5	0	18	0
Sweden		0-0	7-0	—	3	1	1	1	7	2	3

Group II

	Ital.	Lux.	Swi.	Tur.	P	W	D	L	F	A	Pts.
Italy	—			0-0	3	1	2	0	4	0	4
Luxembourg	0-4	—		2-0	3	1	0	2	2	7	2
Switzerland	0-0		—		1	0	1	0	0	0	1
Turkey		3-0		—	3	1	1	1	3	2	3

Group III

	Bel.	Ice.	Neth.	Nor.	P	W	D	L	F	A	Pts.
Belgium	—	4-0	0-0		4	3	1	0	10	0	7
Iceland	0-4	—			3	0	0	3	1	12	0
Netherlands			—	9-0	2	1	1	0	9	0	3
Norway	0-2	4-1		—	3	1	0	2	4	12	2

Group IV

	Alb.	Fin.	E.G.	Rum.	P	W	D	L	F	A	Pts.
Albania	—				2	0	0	2	3	0	0
Finland	1-0	—		1-1	3	1	1	1	2	6	3
E. Germany		5-0	—		1	1	0	0	5	0	2
Rumania	2-0			—	2	1	1	0	3	1	3

Group V

	Eng.	Pol.	Wal.	P	W	D	L	F	A	Pts.
England	—		1-1	2	1	1	0	2	1	3
Poland		—		—	—	—	—	—	—	—
Wales	0-1		—	2	0	1	1	1	2	1

Group VI

	Bul.	N.I.	Port.	Cyp.	P	W	D	L	F	A	Pts.
Bulgaria	—	3-0			2	2	0	0	7	0	4
N. Ireland		—			2	0	0	2	0	4	0
Portugal			—	4-0	2	2	0	0	5	0	4
Cyprus	0-4	1-0	0-1	—	4	1	0	3	1	9	2

Group VII

	Gre.	Spa.	Yugo.	P	W	D	L	F	A	Pts.
Greece	—	2-3		2	0	0	2	2	4	0
Spain		—	2-2	2	1	1	0	5	4	3
Yugoslavia	1-0		—	2	1	1	0	3	2	3

Group VIII

	Cz.	Den.	Scot.	P	W	D	L	F	A	Pts.
Czechoslovakia	—			—	—	—	—	—	—	—
Denmark		—	1-4	2	0	0	2	1	6	0
Scotland		2-0	—	2	2	0	0	6	1	4

Group IX – Winner plays winner of S. America Group III

	Fra.	R.ofI.	USSR							
France	–		1–0		2	1	0	1	2	2	2
Rep. of Ireland	2–1	–	1–2		2	1	0	1	3	3	2
U.S.S.R.			–		2	1	0	1	2	2	2

Host Country: West Germany qualified

SOUTH AMERICA – One qualifier from Groups I and II
Group   I – Colombia, Equador and Uruguay.
Group II – Argentina, Bolivia and Paraguay.
Group III – Chile, Peru and Venezuela. (Winners play winners of Europe Group IX.)
Holder: Brazil qualified

CONCACAF (Central and North America) – One to qualify
Sug-group 1 – Canada, Mexico and USA   *Mexico* qualified for next round
Sub-group 2 – Guatemala and El Salvador.   *Guatemala* qualified for next round
Sub-group 3 – Costa Rica and Honduras.   *Honduras* qualified for next round
Sub-group 4 – Jamaica and Neth. Antilles.   *Neth. Antilles* qualified for next round
Sub-group 5 – Haiti and Puerto Rico.   *Haiti* qualified for next round
Sub-group 6 – Antigua, Surinam and Trinidad.   *Trinidad* qualified for next round

AFRICA – One to qualify
First round

Morocco beat Senegal	0–0 and 2–1
Guinea beat Algeria	5–1 and 0–1
Tunisia beat UAR	1–2 and 2–0
Ivory Coast beat Sierra Leone	2–0 and 1–0
Kenya beat Sudan	0–1 and 2–0
Mauritius beat Madagascar (withdrew)	
Ethiopia beat Tanzania	1–1, 0–0 and 3–0
Zambia beat Lesotho	6–1 and 0–0
Nigeria beat Congo	2–1 and 1–1
Ghana beat Dahomey	2–5 and 5–1
Zaire beat Togo	0–0 and 4–0
Cameroons beat Gabon (withdrew)	

Second round (home and away legs to be played)

Morocco *v* Guinea	
Tunisia *v* Ivory Coast	
Kenya beat Mauritius	3–1 and 2–2
Ethiopia *v* Zambia	
Nigeria *v* Ghana	
Zaire *v* Cameroon	

ASIA – One to qualify
Group A – Israel, Thailand, Malaysia, Philippines, Hong Kong, Korea Rep., Japan and Vietnam Republic.
(The eight will play in pairs to form two sub-groups; each sub-group will then play a one-round league and the winners of each sub-group play a final to decide the Group A winners to play Group B winners for the qualifying place.)

Group B
Sub-group 1 – Australia, Iraq, Indonesia and New Zealand will play a tournament in Australia in March 1973.
Sub-group 2 – Iran, India, Kuwait and Syria will play a tournament in Iran in May 1973. Winners of the two sub-groups to meet home and away to decide the qualifier.